Catarina Lelis

THE IMPACT PLAN
RETHINKING TODAY,
REMAKING TOMORROW,
DESIGNING A BETTER WORLD

BISPUBLISHERS

BIS Publishers
Borneostraat 80-A
1094 CP Amsterdam
The Netherlands
bis@bispublishers.com
www.bispublishers.com

ISBN 978 90 636 9654 2

Contents

Glossary

Assumptions The beliefs and principles that guide our work and that we have about a project, the participants involved, and the way we expect things to evolve.

Beneficiary(ies) The entities, whether targeted or not, that benefit, directly or indirectly, from the project. Any person who gains an advantage and/or profits from something.

Context The circumstances that form the setting for an event, statement, or idea, and in terms of which it can be fully understood. It may include attitudes and expectations by stakeholders, access to documents and sites; it has both a longitudinal (historical, diachronic) and a cross-sectional (concurrent, synchronic) dimension.

Determine To ascertain or establish by research, calculation or gut feeling.

Economic impact Revenue generation, exports, job creation, GDP contributions and similar results.

Environmental impact Changes in biodiversity, pollution levels, water or emissions, etc.

Goal The object of a person's (or group of people's) ambition or effort; an aim or desired result.

Hero A person who is admired for their courage, outstanding achievements, or noble qualities; in mythology, it is a person of superhuman qualities and often semi-divine origin; in this book, it is someone like you and me.

Impact Positive and negative, direct or indirect, intended or unintended, primary and secondary long-term effects produced by and/or attributable to a project. A marked effect or influence.

Indicator Quantitative or qualitative factor, expression or
  variable that provides a simple and reliable means to measure
  achievement, to reflect the changes connected to an intervention,
  or to help assess the performance of a hero.
Outcome The likely or achieved short-term and medium-term
  effects of a project or intervention's outputs. A result or effect that
  is caused by or attributable to the project or intervention.
Persona A persona profile combines user interviews, desk research,
  and other valuable feedback into a single visualization, allowing you
  to collaboratively bring more fidelity to your key personas, develop
  a comprehensive understanding of your current users/beneficiaries,
  and see how to best create solutions for each of them.
Project An activity, intervention, challenge designed to achieve
  specific objectives within specified resources and implementation
  schedules. An individual or collaborative enterprise that is
  carefully planned to achieve a particular goal.
Result(s) A thing that is caused or produced by something else; a
  consequence. It can range from being the output, outcome or impact
  (intended or unintended, positive and/or negative) of a project.
Scenario Text-based stories that form the foundation of a
  storyboard, which adds sketches to illustrate the text.
Social impact The impact on society, people or communities
  resulting from actions, activities, policies and programmes.
Stimulus A spur or incentive, an interesting and exciting quality. A
  thing that arouses activity or energy in someone or something.
Sustainable Development Goals (SDGs) A universal call to action to
  end poverty, protect the planet and ensure that all people enjoy
  peace and prosperity.
Tool A thing used to help perform a job; all heroes have their own
  special tools. A plan can be one of such tools.
Value The importance, worth, or usefulness of something. A valid
  judgment of merit and significance, the main remit of evaluation.

How to use this book

PAGE STRUCTURE

In this book, most of the pages are split into two columns.
Let's take an odd page as example:
- **Inner column**, the main area of contents, where the
  story is told.
- **Outer thinner column**, a space reserved for side
  notes, which aim at complementing whatever is being
  mentioned on the inner one:
  - Links to websites.
  - Additional readings for further info.
  - Music suggestions, supporting the page's
    mindset, or proposed activities. Check the
    playlist on the next page.

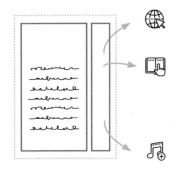

VISUAL HINTS FOR HANDS-ON STUFF

Activities are easily identified:
- A colourful backgound covering most or the entirety
  of the page means there's some practical activity
  in there. Colours are either a light brown (for most
  activities), or the five colours of **The Impact Plan**.
- Icons are used to define the kind of activity:
  - The **swiss army knife** stands for an exercise for
    which you are given a specific brief and indicative
    required time for completion.
  - The **pencil** identifies the page(s) that have been
    left blank for you to note down thoughts, ideas,
    connections and everything precious that pops
    in your head as you advance in anticipating and
    planning your impact.

MOST
ACTIVITIES

THE IMPACT
PLAN
ACTIVITIES

The book's playlist

Scan the QRcode above to access **The Impact Plan Book**'s playlist on YouTube. It has been created as an additional level of meaning. The musics' length is only relevant on those longer than 50 min, which are expected to accompany you until completion of the respective activities.

CHAPTER	ARTIST(S)	MUSIC	LENGTH
Intro	David Bowie	*Heroes*	3:28
	Jamiroquai	*Virtual Insanity*	3:57
1	Bombay Bicycle Club	*Shuffle*	3:45
	Meditation Relax Music	*Alpha Waves*	8:03:20
	Air	*Ce matin la*	3:39
	Nanae Yoshimura	*The Art of Koto Vol. 1*	54:50
	Moby	*Perfect Life*	3:45
	MFSB	*Let's Clean Up The Ghetto*	8:42
	R.E.M.	*Shinny happy people*	3:57
2	The Rolling Stones	*Fortune Teller*	2:20
	The National	*About Today*	4:10
	Stereophonics	*Maybe Tomorrow*	6:03
	LTJ Bukem	*Horizons*	7:57
3	Brooklyn Funk Essentials	*The Creator has a Master Plan*	5:55
	Morelenbaum[2] & Sakamoto	*Casa (full album)*	64:22
	Morcheeba	*Tape Loop*	4:22
4	Kings of Convenience	*I don't know what I can save you from*	4:37
	The Clash	*Should I stay or should I go*	3:09
	Max Richter	*Spring 1 - Recomposed: Vivaldi's Four Seasons*	2:39

Introducing the hero...
Now what?

Now, you're a human being who believes to have crossed the philosophical chasm of repeatedly asking yourself **"What's my purpose on Earth?"**.

Good for you and well done with that! I may have to disappoint you by telling this book is not for you. But please note this crossing is not that easy: after decades of teaching, tutoring, orienting, supervising and hand holding students in higher education settings (the majority of them in postgraduate studies), I have found that only a small portion of these adults has a clear intention in life; in fact, the majority of them is utterly unsure on what they can, may, should or want to do during their advanced studies and, from these, about half is incredibly uncertain about what they can, may, should or want to do when they finish their courses and step into the harsh reality of professional life. This is to say that I believe a great deal of humans (even those who've completed a degree and managed to secure a nice job) have no clear idea what their passions are and what they want to do with their lives. In many cases, the problem is they simply ignore what they're truly good at from a vocational point of view, and what is exactly missing in their capabilities toolkit for them to excel – so that, at some point later in their lives, they can look back and

PLEASURABLE +
MEANINGFUL +
IMPACTFUL

tell a story where they are the heroes of something of relative importance to them: because it involved pleasurable actions, it created meaningful experiences and it led to some kind of impactful (heroic?) event.

Now, what if YOU could be a hero?

[Apologies but a parenthesis is needed for taking proper advantage of the language used to write this book: unlike most other tongues, in English the pronoun YOU alone concentrates in itself the second person singular and plural, addressing the person or persons in either a formal or informal way. Hence, whenever I type YOU hereafter and throughout this book, I will be addressing both the reader as an individual (be it you one of my colleagues or Her Majesty the Queen), and a team, naturally gathering a group of individuals, or formally constituted (be it you a family, or a company or even a nation). We shall now go back to the question...]

What if you could help prevent the occurrence of a tornado, dramatically decreasing the odds for a certain tropical region to be severely devastated and an entire population to be left in destitution? What if I tell you that you can be this kind of hero – *and not just for one day?*

David Bowie
Heroes

You probably heard of *domino* or *ripple effects* before. From a systemic or cybernetics point of view, the expressions serve as metaphors that describe how an action reverberates in the physical and social world. Similarly, but with a pinch of chaos and randomness attached to it, as a result of mathematician Edward Lorenz's observations, in a complex dynamical system, even the smallest action can be amplified and lead to large (negative or positive) consequences, most likely elsewhere in the system. This is due to the sensitive dependence on initial conditions which explains forecast failure, since no variables can be measured with an infinite precision. Known as the *butterfly effect*, it is explained by the theory of chaotic behaviour (or chaos theory) of which a classic example is the potential influence that the flapping of a butterfly's wings can have in the formation and path of a tornado. The one you could help prevent.

Edward Lorenz
Deterministic Nonperiodic Flow

If you watch the news, it's kind of obvious that the world has been having a few problems: increased number of tornados, possibly as a result of climate change, governmental corruption, multiple refugees' crises, unbalanced economic development, radical political and religious views, domestic violence, species' extinction, racism and colourism, deficient mental health care, obsolete educational systems, a crazy pandemic – you name it.

Jamiroquai
Virtual Insanity

Now, what? What are you going to do to not just be a part of the problem? What's your small action that, either linearly or in an organically tortuous or random fashion, is going to have an impact on something or someone and, somehow, help change the world?

You, who read this book

This book aims at helping you find the *journey to impact* of any domestic, mundane, communal, societal problems or causes you care about, and guide you through a mode of thinking and development plan that I call impact-centred. It will orient your problem-solving premisses and will assist you not necessarily in fixing the issue by yourself, but in making a small innovative contribution, which should be expectedly of great relevance to you, for it will make you feel accomplished, fulfilled and, most importantly, a hero. And the interesting aspect of all this is that you can in fact be a hero for more than one day, as you anticipate the continuous reverberance of the impact that your actions (even the very tiny ones, and yes, more than one) may have.

Who exactly are the readers of this book? Who are you? The answer is simple: you are one of those willing to engage with project-based work/activities, both in industry and academia, mostly with keen interest in development, innovation and design-related ventures. Nevertheless, since the tool is so transversally applicable in every domain, you will range from being a Chief Impact Officer or a creative director (in-house or agency-based) to a business entrepreneur, from a freelance lawyer to a healthcare student.

And whose needs does this book meet?

Yours, if you are facing a pool of different possible projects/briefs to engage in, and from which you need to choose only one, either by discarding the others, or by postponing them. An evaluation of risks and priorities tends to be a common approach for selection purposes, but what **The Impact Plan** does, what no other tool or support to thinking system achieves, is that it reveals the combination of perils, skills and priorities with desires and the perception/anticipation of possible impact.

In higher education, **The Impact Plan** will be essential to those students taking final project modules. Hence, in an academic context, the main audience are students on advanced undergraduate and postgraduate level. Every Design, Communication and Media, Innovation, Business and Entrepreneurship and every course where Challenge or Project-Based Learning is a common teaching approach (in both final years of UG studies and PG programmes), will find this book and its tools of great use. It will also serve researchers who may find themselves surrounded by challenging multiple projects, either in the potential role of principal investigator or as a team member. You may not be able to go for all (projects), so I think **The Impact Plan** may give you a hand in choosing the one(s). Similarly, in some industries, professionals often receive several briefs simultaneously, having to prioritise or choose the one to work on at that moment, usually by considering aspects such as budget, time frame, strength, and longevity of the relationship with the client, but also the project itself, its message, challenge, values, and purpose.

These situations involve difficult decisions and anxious moments, due to the lack of:
1. a supporting and defining framework for said decision, and
2. a system for reflecting on how each of the possible projects to choose from can become a more or less pleasurable, meaningful, and impactful action in the short, mid, and long run.

PLEASURABLE, MEANINGFUL AND IMPACTFUL Not just for the user, not just for the client, not just for the team, but for a wider community too, possibly for humanity and the planet. Therefore, potentially scaling the impact to unexpected levels, given that often individuals, teams, and boards are not fully aware of a project's ramifications. And let's not forget that life is an unpredictable journey with its multiple experiences and projects. So, to clarify the utility of **The Impact Plan,** besides the academic context (in which the tool was born), the commercial environment of companies, the non-profit mindset of charities working on societal issues, climate change, and cleaning up the world, this book may well bring some (humble) orientation to the other social institutions of our lives, those abstract fields of values and rules, such as family.

So, thank you!

Thank you for buying or borrowing or stealing this book. Our publisher may not like the last option, but the truth is, if you had to nick this book from somewhere, most likely it was because you want to read it. Which you are! So, again, thank you:

- for reading this book,
- for being a hands-on kind of person,
- for trying to find your vocational home turf, and the impact of what you do,
- for conceiving yourself as an innovative hero – even if just for one day.

How the book is organised

Although the language is deemed not to be complex nor to follow any specific industry or domain related jargon, a small glossary has been prepared for your convenience. You must have bumped into it already.

As for the main body of contents... OK, let's admit it: given the way I've been introducing **The Impact Plan** and its spectacular qualities – which you will confirm by the end of the book – I'd like to confess I have a little bit of a hero's profile too. In fairness, I also have a bigger purpose, which is to disseminate **The Impact Plan** so that others can use it to positively change the world. That's why I organised this book following the famous monomyth, widely known as the Hero's Journey:

Joseph Campbel
The Hero with a Thousand Faces

Grounded in the work of Joseph Campbel — who hammered out the metaphor for the journey of transformation that heroes in every time and place seem to share — Scott Allison, Professor of Psychology at the University of Richmond, US, says "hero stories illuminate your true purpose in four ways:

You will go on a journey;
You will grow from adversity;
You will assemble a team of allies, and
You will give back to society".

Chapter 1 introduces you to the **Impact Journey**. It starts with a quick overview of the relevance of anticipating impact, namely from an ordinary world point of view. The 2030 agenda by the United Nations and its 17 goals for sustainable development are used as a north star in **The Impact Plan**, but readers are nudged toward thinking beyond these and beyond their set deadline. Since Purpose has become an essential expression for many non-governmental and private, commercial entities – and impact cases are being used as metrics of success – some dilemmas (for example, COVID-19 and its impact on individuals' generalised forms of freedom) will be introduced so you can meditate on the possible conflict of interest and/or alignment between individual wellbeing, the call to being a hero, and the common-good.

Chapter 2, **Designing from Adversities**, looks into the Double Diamond (by the Design Council UK) as an innovation project framework, and elaborates on where **The Impact Plan** would sit within it. I argue that there is a moment of pre-engagement with a project taking place before the first stage in this model, a moment I call the *Determine* phase, where individuals and teams are still unable to Discover since the step of choosing which project to go for (namely when there are a few under consideration, which is not uncommon) is still to be taken. **The Impact Plan** introduces the need and awareness to such an important stage where individuals would focus on identifying the main WHYs of those projects under consideration, where some decision-making is already taking place, much of which will have decisive implications during the project's remaining stages. In this chapter, different modes of thinking, heuristics, and the exercises of forecasting and backcasting are explored in order to anticipate and plan scenarios of impact.

Chapter 3 will help you **Assemble your Allies and Achieve a Result**. This is the chapter in which the tool and its *modus operandi* is explained in detail. Your own possible Hero's Journey will be elucidated. First, the tool is broken down, and its close connection with different moments in time, in which impact can be anticipated, is presented. The concept of Beneficiary is explained. Then the cards are introduced by category, looking at both their stimuli, which are supposed to be used as metrics, and the scenarios of impact they belong to. The book also includes **The Impact Plan** canvas broken down into six autonomous boards. The purpose of the tool is to work more as a heuristic for rapid and easy assessment of impact – and its use is seen as mostly helpful at the very early stage of choosing which brief or project to take on. In this sense, **The Impact Plan** can work as a creative sanctuary, as it protects the user from influences, from all the other stuff that is constantly coming at you.

Chapter 4, **You, Yourself and Humanity,** takes you to the deserved moment of showcasing the potential impact your choice may have, providing you with the tools to build a cogent rationale that, I hope, will solidly convince both your Me and your Myself, but also your managers, clients, teachers or investors. **The Impact Plan**'s ecosystem is also detailed so you can get a better sense of where you may use it throughout your journey as a hero. Finally, you'll find a few considerations on the challenges of *Giving Back to Society*, which is the ultimate goal.

Going on the
Impact Journey

All the world is made of faith, and trust, and pixie dust.
[Peter Pan]

It all started with my postgraduate students, in London. I realised
that when initiating them to the very first quest moments that would
expectedly result in their Master's Project formation, most of them were
unable to articulate a problem-based question; I also found that this was
because they couldn't think of a Problem they thought they might be
able to solve. The reason Problem is written with capital P is because the
Problem was THE Problem. The conceptual boundaries for what could be

United Nations
The 17 Sustainable
Development Goals

considered a Problem were not clear. In fact, the world was already dealing with the few Problems mentioned before, most of them massive societal issues that one individual alone could not solve by him or herself — let alone during the length of a Masters course. Around 2016, the UN's 17 Sustainable Development Goals from the 2030 Agenda became widely known. These were aimed at tackling big, fat, and ugly Problems. Anything else looked just like a satellite or minor issue, the resolution of which would be either a follow-up or the mere consequence of having solved the big, fat, and ugly ones.

Well... I've been tempted to say that no, not really, that's not the way it works. What if we were to invert things by addressing the satellite minor issues first, getting them sorted and creating a collection of solutions that can possibly and somehow contribute to the resolution of something big, fat, and ugly? "I mean, what annoyingly pisses you off — like every single day?", I would insist. So, very timidly and with careful reservations, my students started listing all kinds of small Problems they were dealing with in their everydayness and which, for one reason or another, were contributing to their discomfort, anxiety, and frustration. The morning seems to be the period of the day in which individuals face some of the most exasperating events, like the inability to find the right pair of socks or having to deal with fox faeces on the outdoor doormat. Accompanied with some incentivising prompts and follow-up questions, I found that these satellite minor issues — which, in principle, wouldn't deserve dissemination because of how minor they are and how embarrassing they can be...

- contribute to how individuals face the rest of their day, by simultaneously setting down, only to a certain degree, the expectations for the days to come, and
- were common to more than one individual in the same classroom; the one to first acknowledge one of such issues was rapidly followed by several "So do I!"s.

I then asked them:

1. if they still thought the minor Problem they had mentioned was only theirs — to which most answered "probably not".
2. If they could conceive their Problem as part of a bigger one (cultural, political, environmental, etc.) — to which the answers were "absolutely, yes".
3. if they thought they could help solving it — to which they answered, "not sure, I guess so".
4. and how they thought the Problem might be tackled — to which answers varied immensely, although the majority involved some kind of hi-tech-based new product or digitally mediated service or a different approach on the way we communicate in society.

Hence, the timing for this book sounds just about right. The world needs to be saved; the UN set the timer for its goals to be achieved, admitting that the defining three pillars of sustainable development — economic, social and environmental — are currently fairly imbalanced; the advancements in technology and the integration of digital features in our lives have increased dramatically; people are happier when they follow a challenging, developmental, and meaningful direction — their impact journey. But they're even happier if they can have all this with the least possible effort.

Dolce far niente while saving the World

So, as mentioned, the United Nations came up with an agenda for sustainable development that includes a set of goals to end poverty, protect the planet, and ensure prosperity for all, claiming that "everyone needs to do their part: governments, the private sector, civil society and people like you". And by "people like you" they basically mean you don't need to be either a superhero (alien or not) or a multimillionaire. In fact, you don't even need to be extremely involved on or eager to saving the world because the UN has put together a list of actions for anyone like you to take in their everyday life, therefore easily contributing to a sustainable future: "The Lazy Person's Guide to Saving the World". Interestingly, the first context in which lazy people like you can contribute to such an honourable mission is — guess what! — being a hero from your couch!

United Nations
The Lazy Person's Guide to Saving the World

OK — so, what exactly is the UN telling us? My interpretation is that one can easily be a hero by being... lazy. American author and abolitionist (but also one of the most influential women of the 19th century) Harriet Beecher Stowe said "Human nature is above all things lazy". One hundred and fifty years have passed, and things didn't seem to have changed much for the hopeless lazy humans — despite the start of a new millennium. In 2015 a group of researchers from the Simon Fraser University in Canada confirmed that humans are biologically wired to be lazy and that, even when performing very basic moves such as walking our subconscious nervous system continuously fine-tunes movements to keep energy costs low. Think of our ancestors: they had to conserve energy to compete for resources and to fight or flee both enemies and predators. Expending effort on anything other than short-term advantage could seriously compromise their survival.

Cognitive ergonomics has been showing we preserve some kind of laziness in the form of mental shortcuts (heuristics) without which we wouldn't be able to learn, nor to know or understand the world, for that matter. These heuristics are responsible for all the unconscious

and automatic (lazy) behaviours we
have or actions we perform that simply
allow us to optimise certain activities
without having to think too much and
over and over again. Driving a car is a
good example: an experienced driver
doesn't consciously think on when to
press the clutch pedal, nor does he/she
make a detailed plan on the sequence of speeds to be used when
driving from A to B. They simply drive, some of them pretty well
and pretty fast. That's because they're mostly resorting to their
cognitive shortcuts — in other words, they're being super lazy! So,
the bottom line is, really, the lazier you are, the better you will be at
something. And all this to say that by calling "lazy" to people like
you, the UN is not putting you under injurious or underrated labels
such as slothful, lethargic, or inert; rather, it acknowledges human
nature as it is, admitting that most of us are keen on optimising our
surroundings so that we spend the less possible energy (hence, being
efficient) whilst obtaining a desired or intended result (hence, being
effective). What else do you need if you want to change the world?

Daniel Kahneman
Thinking, Fast and Slow

The trouble is that saving the world may take a while and, according
to psychologist and author Neel Burton, most of us are not that
inclined to invest in a return that is both distant and uncertain. He
also defends that humans are poor anticipators and that "a kind of
hedonistic calculus should be applied to determine which things
are most likely to result in the greatest pleasure over time". So, for
lazy heroes like you and me (and the rest of us) to move a finger
to save the world we ought to get a clear notion of what's in it for
us — and that means some kind of not-taking-too-long immediate
gratification that makes up for the loss of comfort.

Neel Burton
*Hide and Seek: The
Psychology of Self-
Deception*

How super-lazy are you?

1. Type "The Lazy Person's Guide to Saving the World" in your browser's search field and then choose the UN's result, which should be the first one on the list.
2. Scroll down and browse over the four (4) contexts of laziness to find the many things you can do to make an impact.
3. Pick three (3) from each context and write them down on the next page. Choose wisely: select only those you truly know you'd be able to engage with. And don't cheat by picking those you have already implemented in your everyday life — Don't be that lazy!
4. Now, think of the impact each of your actions may have on you, personally and professionally. For example, if you decide you will let your hair dry naturally, how does that impact your appearance? How will you feel about that? What side effects might that bring? What other routines could be affected? And how often would you have to deal with them? Do question all your 12 selected actions.
5. Finally, allocate a score to each one of them in terms of their impact on you. Use the following impact score scale:

   -2 (very negative impact) | -1 (some negative impact)

   0 (neutral impact)

   +1 (some positive impact) | +2 (very positive impact)

45 mn   **Bombay Bicycle Club**
Shuffle

LEVEL OF LAZINESS	TO DOS TO SAVE THE WORLD	IMPACT ON MY DAILY LIFE	IMPACT SCORE
1			
1			
1			
2			
2			
2			
3			
3			
3			
4			
4			
4			

Purpose Disruptors
www.purposedisruptors.org

The Good Life 2030
www.
goodlife2030.earth

Common-good and humanity-centredness

The Purpose Disruptors are a network of advertising professionals working together to reshape their industry so it can contribute to tackling climate change. In 2021 they launched The Good Life 2030 initiative which aims at reclaiming 2030 and giving a new meaning to what *good life* is or can be. Their main question is:

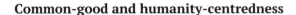

WHAT IF THE FUTURE
WAS WORTH LOOKING
FORWARD TO?

Basically, they seek answers to what if the future was something we could think of without concern? What if the vision of the future could be more captivating than upsetting? What if we all could "live more connected and meaningful lives"? What if said future was actually good? But in a way it could be good and pleasurable for all! In a way where the capital common-good would be the planet. According to the Stanford Encyclopaedia of Philosophy, the common good refers to the resources that the individuals, members of a community, provide to all other members to fulfil their duty of care for certain interests that they all have in common. In a modern liberal democracy these are "the road system; public parks; police protection and public safety; courts and the judicial system; public schools; museums and cultural institutions; public transportation; civil liberties, such as the freedom of speech and the freedom of association; the system of property; clean air and clean water; and national defence". What about all this being good for all, plus for the planet we all live on?

The sceptics would probably call it *utopia*, but we may have reached some kind of saturation moment in which idyllic and heroic thoughts are necessary, anticipating a good-looking happy future for all. When we try to visualise things that are seemingly odd or difficult to attain, we naturally shift our thinking mode from vertical (which includes selective, analytical, and sequential logical processes) to lateral, where we acknowledge the possibility of big, fat and ugly Problems unfolding in a completely different and unforeseeable way. And then, as said by Eduard de Bono, who coined the term in his book *Lateral Thinking*, "suddenly, a surprisingly simple solution emerges".

Eduard de Bono
Lateral Thinking: Creativity
Step by Step

The world — the same one that is queuing to be saved — asks for some humanity- and planetary-centred lateral thinking, pondering and action. As professionals, designers seem to have been doing this since they became aware of their deontological burden toward humans and the planet. Human-centred design approaches focus on understanding the point of view and the needs of those who experience a problem. But in this case the centredness must be much broader since we're not dealing with just a segment of humans with a specific problem which one can centre on; rather, we're addressing all humans, regardless their specific needs and, on top of that, the planet, which includes all its natural idiosyncrasies that go beyond humans.

One of the findings of The Good Life 2030 initiative was that, despite the high levels of anxiety in relation to the future, "people aren't emotionally connecting to 2030". It seems that the jargon that's being used in the most diverse forms of communication is not that relatable, and the big, fat, and ugly Problems to be tackled do go way beyond humans and their understanding. Augmenting the common good and improving the quality of life for all must be achieved by all but, again, for most individuals, such commitment becomes much clearer and obvious when they foresee the domestic benefits it will bring them.

Visualising a good life in the future

What would the future look like in 10 years' time should life be truly good for all?

Write or draw your ONE idea that would represent a good life in each of the three contexts on the right. It doesn't matter if your ideals of *good life* sound like impossible dreams or even infantile deviations. What's important is that you identify WHAT *good life* means to you.

As for the HOW, you may find useful making a list of the conflicts and obstacles you may have to face and overcome; the possible concessions you may have to commit to and the tensions you will experience. You want to be aware of these so you can explore the most positive and hassle-free aproaches.

And, you may need a nice couple of hours to get a clear vision of a good life in the future... So, take your time!

Simon Sinek
Start with Why:
How Great Leaders
Inspire Everyone to
Take Action

SIMON SINEK SAYS WE SHOULD START WITH THE WHY, BUT THIS TIME (AND THIS TIME ONLY) WE WILL LEAVE IT TO THE END.

Meditation Music
Alpha Waves
8:03:20

WHAT
WOULD A GOOD LIFE MEAN

In your personal life	In your professional life	In society and nature

HOW
MIGHT YOU ACHIEVE IT? (THINK LATERALLY, NOT LITERALLY)

In your personal life	In your professional life	In society and nature

Back to purpose — or to something called *ikigai*

If you managed to visualise WHAT a good life in the future could be, and then imagined HOW you might get there, the question that remains to be answered is WHY. I agree it may not be that easy to find the WHY. Let me give you a hand.

Ikigai (/ˈɪkɪɡʌɪ/) is a Japanese concept that brings together the terms *iki*, which means *life*, and *gai*, which means *worthwhile* or *benefit*. When combined, these terms mean something that could be translated as what gives your life worth or meaning, whatever makes you get out of bed each day in eager anticipation. To some extent the concept of *ikigai* is like the French *raison d'être* — the purpose for being — which changes throughout our lives.

Hector Garcia & Francesc Miralles
The Ikigai Journey

In their book "The Ikigai Journey", Hector Garcia and Francesc Miralles propose a framework made up of four components to help people find their *ikigai*. It is grounded on the thought that it is an illusion to believe that our purpose in life "is something magical we are destined to find accidentally or through a revelation (...) Nothing new or exciting will happen if you do not take steps to make it happen" — they say. They also add a quote by Donald Kendall, American businessman and political adviser, who served as CEO of Pepsi Cola and PepsiCo for about 15 years, and who brilliantly said:

THE ONLY PLACE WHERE SUCCESS COMES BEFORE WORK IS IN THE DICTIONARY

The four components for people to find their *ikigai* are:

- What you love
- What you are good at
- What you can be paid for
- What the world needs

By listing the answers to all the above, Garcia and Miralles's model allows you to find your passion, profession, vocation and mission — in short, your *ikigai*. It's quite simple, provided your four lists overlap at some point. Once you identify common themes in both what you love and what you're good at you'll get a clearer sense of what your passions are. If there are any shared elements in both what you're good at and what you can be paid for, you'll probably find your ideal profession. If you can identify repeated themes between what you can be paid for and what the world needs, you'll get a sense of what your vocation is. And once you find the recurrent themes in what the world needs and what you love, you'll know your mission.

♫⊕
Air
Ce matin la

Alright, let's recapitulate so that we can get this right before we go any further:
- The world urgently needs to be saved due to a lot of pervasive big, fat and ugly Problems,
- we're all potentially heroes in the sense that we can make a difference, but...
- we're all hardwired to be lazy! Nevertheless...
- we're all driven by a selfish need to understand what we will get from our saving-the-world actions, and
- we're all more or less inspired by some kind of purpose, to which the Japanese call *ikigai*.

Exactly, you nailed it!

What's your *ikigai?* Can you find it in less than one hour?

♥ **WHAT YOU LOVE**	This should include all things that make you feel good, happy and fulfilled.

WHAT YOU'RE GOOD AT	This will highlight your talents, what you know you can master, both with the skills you currently have and with the skills you may need to develop in the short-term.

WHAT YOU CAN BE PAID FOR	How can you make a living and make money? Can you use any of your talents or knowledge? Note that what you can be paid for may differ from what you're good at.

WHAT THE WORLD NEEDS	List the needs of your family, friends, neighbours, colleagues, country or even an external community somewhere remote. The needs you sincerely believe you could engage with.

♥ **WHAT YOU LOVE**	Yes, revisit all things that make you feel good and happy, now to overlap with the list above.

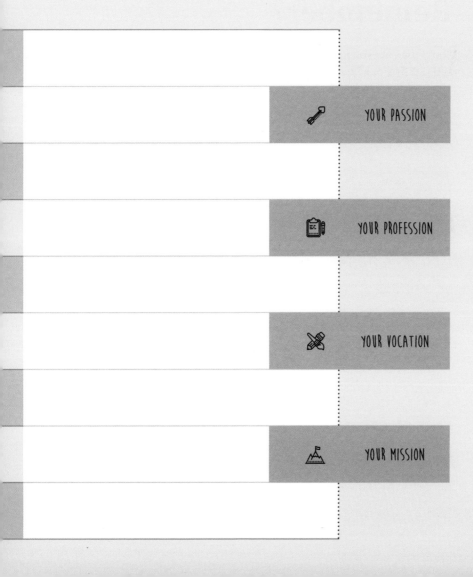

Nanae Yoshimura
The Art of Koto Vol. 1
54:50

YOUR PASSION

YOUR PROFESSION

YOUR VOCATION

YOUR MISSION

20 mn

Moby
Perfect Life

Visualising a good life in the future...

Remember?

Using the data you just assembled, you may now be better equipped to answer WHY. Why would you bother with reaching a good life in the future?

WHY WOULD YOU BOTHER WITH REACHING A GOOD LIFE IN THE FUTURE?		
For your personal life	For your professional life	For society and nature

Being heroes in the world of brands

The first lockdown imposed by COVID-19 has already brought some awareness to the way we live and, most importantly, the way we should be living. Impactful consequences on people's lives ranged from absurdly negative, such as losing their jobs and their loved ones, to highly positive, as in having more time for their family and finding new hobbies. The industry had to adjust to the new norm of a worldwide society buying more online while stepping way less into brick-and-mortar stores and facilities — which, to some sectors, and for a while, meant little to zero profit (take as examples the inappropriately ventilated underground dance clubs, or even the until then hyper-busy airline companies). Institutions and brands across the whole industry spectrum had to step back and rethink their approaches, their business models, their customer services. Many had to reconsider their purpose.

In 2021, Interbrand launched Heartbeat, its Human Truths platform which looks at "what it means to be human and the issues that face us all in our everyday lives". As part of their work, they found that, after the radical change provoked by the pandemic, the re-evaluation we're all going through has created room for new experiences that the majority of people have found enjoyable. This is a big insight for businesses of all sectors, since the changes that had to be implemented in what we thought would be a temporary phase, in some cases may have come to stay for good, and in others may have drawn attention to the need for urgent and/or frequent redesigns. After surveying 7000 consumers across seven countries in the world, Capgemini consultancy reports that brands have been

Interbrand
interbrand.com/heartbeat/

Capgemini
Why purpose-led
organizations are winning
consumers' hearts

realising that their audiences are much more sensitive to companies whose reason for being goes way beyond profit and which instead reflect something aspirational, something that positively impacts society and the planet. This is even more true at a time when humanity is recovering from such a shabby health crisis. The main findings of Capgemini's work are:

- Consumers have high expectations of companies and brands said to be purpose-led, and most believe private companies have an increasingly bigger responsibility toward society.
- They will reward through emotional connections and engagement those that contribute to overcoming the crisis installed by the pandemic.
- They also expect to get clear and consistent evidence on how companies and brands live their purpose.

How a brand translates its purpose into action depends on its specific goals, needs, and values, which should be embodied in the experiences it provides to both customers and employees. Over the past years, many large brand companies have announced they would align to some of the UN's SDGs. Their claims are they want to make a positive impact, to some extent making up for the disastrous situation the environment currently faces, and which many of these companies contributed to.

For example, Nestlé, PepsiCo and Unilever are among the ones that have been committed to making 100% of their packaging recyclable, reusable or compostable by 2025. In 2021 Tide launched the #TurntoCold campaign, after discovering that doing your laundry in cold water can reduce energy usage by up to 90 percent, therefore reducing greenhouse gas emissions. Sephora has developed its diversity, equity, and inclusion platform, Sephora Stands, whose main goal is to encourage individuals to see their inner beauty.

The cosmetics brand does this by supporting communities' differences and the beauty of life, by inviting people (like you) to preserve the planet. Together with consumers, Brands for Good, an initiative promoted by Sustainable Brands, have identified the Nine Most Impactful Sustainable Behaviours for brands, to get some guidance toward driving a culture of sustainable living. They have been working closely with giant companies to show smaller ones that a lot can be done by authentically, consistently, and meaningfully communicating the purpose behind a brand or product.

Brands for Good
sbbrandsforgood.com

In fact, it may look like being a hero in industry is limited to those 1) holding magnificent branded empires or 2) listed in Dow Jones. Fortunately, not quite. Products like the 2030 Calculator, powered by agency FARM and winner of a D&AD Impact Pencil, are excellent examples of solutions that inspire small businesses and local brands to make an impact, creating awareness and fostering transparency. It is "the first tool that allows brands to quickly and easily quantify the carbon footprint of the products they manufacture, using a common universal scoring system".

2030 Calculator
planetloyalty.com

The B-Corp Movement is another sort of bootcamp for industry heroes which is worth mentioning. Their motto is "We won't stop until all business is a force for good". For-profit companies certified with this private B stamp acquire the status of a Benefit corporation. The B basically means that these businesses are driven by both purpose and profit, whilst meeting high standards of verified performance, accountability, and transparency on factors such as employee rights and benefits, charitable giving, supply chain fair practices, and both controlled and sustainable input materials. They have these B Labs around the world, making sure there are "standards, policies, tools, and programs that shift the behaviour, culture, and structural underpinnings of capitalism", aiming at addressing society's most critical and current issues. And their annual fees are not that high (naturally proportional to revenues)...

B-Corp
www.
bcorporation.net

Some brands, such as non-profits and charities, navigate through different seas. Universities are a great example, namely because they are inclined to naturally contribute to society, if not by other means, at the very least by producing educated and developed humans that tend to dispense some time thinking about and investigating the world around them.

UNAI
www.
un.org/en/
academicimpact

The United Nations Academic Impact (UNAI) is an initiative that "unites institutions of higher education around the shared goal of using scientific inquiry, academic research, and education to further the realisation of United Nations goals and mandates", including the promotion and protection of human rights, equal access to education, conflict resolution, and planetarian sustainability. Each member institution is responsible for actively demonstrating support of at least one of the UNAI principles or one of the Sustainable Development Goals each year. In fact, in principle, higher education institutions have the basic conditions to help the UN in achieving the Sustainable Development Goals, since they serve as incubators of new solutions to the global challenges the world faces. UNAI promotes specialised hubs for each of the SDGs, doing cutting edge research with its members. And increasingly, in the academic context, funding for research is approved and released based on the potential and anticipated impact the research may have in society. This being said, universities and colleges also need to find their brand's *raison d'être*!

Simon Sinek says, "True purpose is lived from the inside out". And, we mentioned this already, he also says we should start with the WHY. His Golden Circle model is based on evidence that shows that connecting with people by having a clear Purpose (and through shared beliefs and values) can lead to growth.

Since the era of Purpose and its business case have come to stay for a while and are so well documented, companies have come to realise that giving their brands a genuine purpose is not such a waste of time; rather, it may signify boosting profits and staff morale.

Also, many branding professionals (designers, strategists) have been relying on a very simple tool called the Brand Purpose Butterfly to identify a brand's WHY. It basically is a hyper-summarised version of the *ikigai* framework proposed by Garcia and Miralles: two chained ellipses that cross over in the middle, which is precisely where your brand's purpose should appear.

If you have a brand and are in search of its purpose, you may want to get your hands onto the next activity.

40 mn

MFSB
*Let's Clean Up The
Ghetto*

Identifying a brand's purpose

To find the purpose behind your business, you can use either or both models: Synek's Golden Circle and the Brand Purpose Butterfly.

I'd suggest you use both, starting with the latter. Once you find your brand's purpose, which is roughly its WHY, transfer it to Sinek's inner circle.

BRAND PURPOSE BUTTERFLY

In the top wing you should write what the world (or the sector within which you operate) needs. On the wing at the bottom write what's special and unique about your brand — in short, what the brand is truly good at.

Your Brand Purpose lies in the intersection, right in the middle. It brings the contents of the two wings together, by clarifying how the latter can contribute to the former.

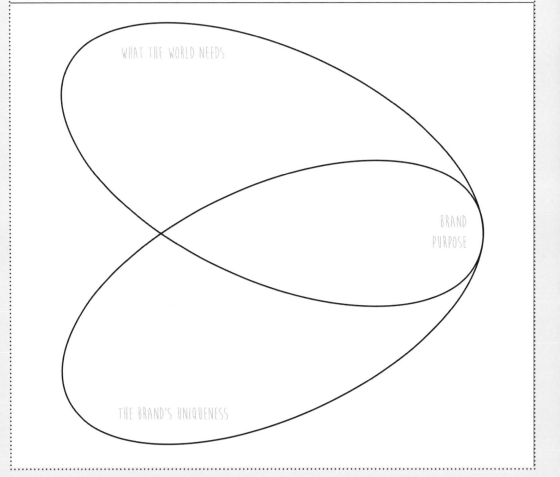

WHAT THE WORLD NEEDS

BRAND PURPOSE

THE BRAND'S UNIQUENESS

SINEK'S GOLDEN CIRCLE

Start with WHY, the inner circle, which is the Brand Purpose you just identified on the left. Is it clear? — that is fundamental for you to proceed to the next level.

If yes, move to the circle in the middle to answer HOW. You should list processes and methods that will define the path to be followed for the company to fulfil its purpose and achieve its objectives.

In the outward circle you'll clarify the WHAT, the product or service that you deliver to your audiences, that helps you achieve your purpose and make a heroic contribution to the world.

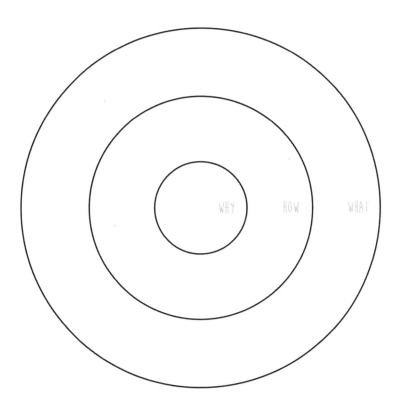

Pleasurable <> Meaningful <> Impactful

The increasing awareness around mental health issues in the last decades — and the acceptance these health problems can be as letal as lung cancer or diabetes — has shed light to the importance of generic wellbeing and mindfulness. The NHS, the UK's National Health System, has made available a webpage on "How to be happier", filled with tips and multimedia contents to support individuals in pursuing this goal. If we all could live a *good life* (in the future), we'd all be happier.

R.E.M.
Shinny happy people

One of the tips is that we should enjoy ourselves. Pleasurable and simple activities like "having a soak in the bath or meeting up with friends for coffee can all improve your day". The list then goes on, focusing on pleasurable activities that involve production and in which we're good at (e.g. writing, drawing, dancing, singing, etc), as good ways to enjoy ourselves and get a sense of achievement. It can also happen at work (if you like your job)! At some point you're so into what you're doing, that time goes by and you don't even notice. You don't feel hungry, you don't feel tired (although you may be inexplicably exhausted) and the *comfort room* is often forgotten until you can't manage it any longer. You simply fail to remember any other responsibilities, like walking the dog or picking up your kids from school. You're going through what Hungarian psychologist Mihaly Csikszentmihalyi called *flow*, or the *optimal experience*: "I have called [it] flow, because many of the respondents described the feeling when things were going well as an almost automatic, effortless, yet highly focused state of consciousness".

Mihaly Csikszentmihalyi
Flow: The Psychology of Optimal Experience

Our consumerism and industrialised culture have shaped the way we understand life and work leading to two kinds of working people-like-you: those that work to live, and those that live to work. In most of our models for living, we tend to conceptualise work as a hassle, labour that involves great effort and little enjoyment. The opposite of work is understood as rest and pleasure, consisting of activities such as relaxing on the couch while watching TV, socialising at the pub, shopping, going to the spa or on holidays somewhere far from home (and from work). One may say they all configure as those eventful things that make us feel incredibly lazy... So, we should also agree that what these activities have in common is that they're all generally superficial, non-challenging and passive.

However, we've already seen that we can contribute toward saving the world by being naturally lazy. Maybe a pleasurable activity such as a soak in the bath is not the best example on how we can contribute to any of the United Nations SDGs, but a pleasurable one such as meeting up with friends for coffee may involve small little actions that help reducing gas emissions — cycling to the meeting point — or that contribute toward a fairer world — choosing a coffee brand committed to providing decent work conditions to its workers.

Imagine you can experience pleasurable moments through deeper, demanding, and bustling activities. Sounds great, right? Sounds like *flow*! Imagine yourself being rewarded for what you love, what you're good at, and for contributing to what the world undoubtedly needs. What would this mean to you? And what would this mean to anyone benefiting from anything produced with such a high level of engagement and excitement? Wouldn't it be a pleasurable and meaningful experience? On the other hand, do you think this could be considered an optimal experience?

Well, I tend to disagree with Mihaly's on this one. Purely due to semantics, if we concur that *optimal* means *ideal* (as in a preferable projection of the future), I think that for an experience, activity, or project to be optimal you need not only the pleasurability and the meaningfulness but also to anticipate the positive impact of the outcomes of what you do.

It will certainly put a bigger smile on your lazy heroic face.

Notes, thoughts, drawings, ideas ...

Don't let them escape. Keep them on this page, you may need them for later. You can also stick some post-its if you struggle with the space below — or if you're proficient in dealing with several *layers* of information.

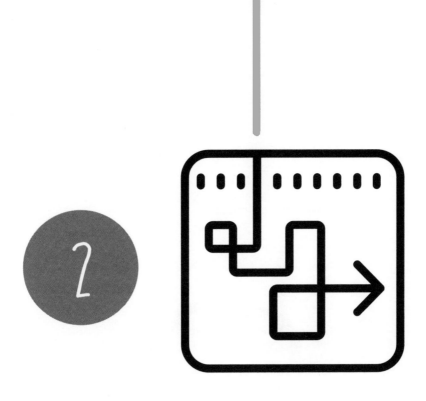

Designing
from Adversity

What makes the desert beautiful is that somewhere it hides a well...
[The Little Prince]

In the previous chapter we got to know the hero and identify with him/her before the journey begins. We had to do that since you must feel like you could get into this hero's boots, and because it is important that you relate to the idea of being a hero, so you can experience the journey of **The Impact Plan** through a hero's pair of eyes, glasses or binoculars. Once the journey begins, looking into your purpose while standing in the comfort

Eyes, glasses or binoculars?

of your "Ordinary World" gives you the opportunity to identify with your hero's drives, questions and problems, while realising the unique characteristics and flaws that make of you the normal, flesh-and-bone — and yes, lazy! —person we gladly got to meet.

But the main feature of the monomyth is that there is no need for a hero if there is no threat, confrontation, or spectacular adventure in the horizon. What makes the hero a hero is the remarkable moment when they overcome the adversity that has originally disrupted the amenity of their Ordinary World, the moment in which they restore life into its ordinariness — which is usually an evolution of the previous establishments, becoming then the new normality. Your call to adventure starts when you realise that the future is worth looking forward to, that there may be a good life project for you and, potentially, for all. It starts when you apprehend and conceive a challenge or quest that must be undertaken, when you or someone (or something) throws the Ordinary World off balance. It starts when you, the hero, roll up your sleeves and acknowledge what's at stake in case the challenge is ignored or rejected.

This book would come to an end right here, right now, should heroes have an easy and highly effective system for hero-challenge allocation. Imagine a life where you only had one problem to solve at a time. And if said life were not to exist, imagine there was a ticketing system through which you, queueing up with all other heroes, would pick a sequential coupon that would objectively state THE challenge you were expected to solve. Pretty much like what Ethan Hunt and his Impossible Missions Force get before the tape/disc/file self-destructs in five seconds. Just imagine! You would never have to go through that miserable shilly-shally feeling of "which-problem-should-I-tackle-first?" because there would be a superior entity or some kind of overarching governing system making that decision for you. Sounds like a bliss. You know why? Because many times — in fact, most of them — the hero, whose purpose is more or less well defined, needs to choose between two or more conflicting calls which are, somehow and allegedly, aligned to his/her purpose.

So, which call should the hero nail first? If not randomly assigned and if quest allocation is not controlled by this god-like intelligence, what metrics or criteria should the hero rely on to decide on the right journey for that particular moment in life?

Let's not forget the laziness and the fact that humans, very humanely, are not willing to make changes, usually preferring the safe haven of their known ordinary world. The insecurities around both changing behaviours and the sacrifices, risks or likelihood

of failure any changes may bring along are sufficiently disturbing and enough for sleeves to be rolled down again. This is, in fairness, the first adversity heroes like you must overcome. And this is precisely when a Mentor comes to stage to provide insight, advice, training, or even "magical" resources to help us build the confidence necessary to face the threshold of the adventure and the journey's ordeals.

Learning from Design

Design is a transformational and inspirational humanist system that constantly shapes the world around us, bridging efficiency, efficacy and experience, balancing technical, commercial and human considerations, for the humans.

Design is the ultimate promoter of the craft of thinking and of having ideas; it is a creativity enabler that benignly infects those around with the enthusiasm and the passion inherent to whom (or what) is equipped with many making-oriented tools to solve a wide range of problems. Geraint Rees, Dean of the Faculty of Life Sciences and a Professor of Cognitive Neurology at University College London says "Design is a much bigger subject than science and has greater impact", and ethnographer and social anthropologist Sarah Pink once said, "design is inevitably an engagement with the future". In fact, often focused on the future, the work of design involves solving problems for multiple stakeholders in a complex changing world.

Design is also considered as a sector in its own right. It is a specialised, professional economic activity performed by trained and qualified practitioners, and it is also a tool for business and organisational growth at the highest strategic level. Moreover, design also encompasses sustainable and responsible behaviour contributing positively to an innovative society and improved quality of life.

Design for growth & prosperity
https://op.europa.eu/en/ home

The Design Council is an independent charity and the UK Government's advisor on design, whose mission is "to champion great design that improves lives and makes things better". Its contributions are evidence that design is an inherently interdisciplinary field deeply involved with humans' basic needs and the concreteness of the changing and demanding world around humans. In light of this, it would not be unreasonable to say that the expression "human-centred design" is highly tautological since, in my view, design is not design if it is not constitutionally and implicitly humanity-centred. Which we know it is. In fact, it can (and should) even go beyond humanity...

With this kind of mindset and toolkit, what better mentor could a hero ask for?

Determine: the missing D word

In 2005, the Design Council developed the 'Double Diamond' model (DD) to illustrate general activities and the overall process common to all designers. It intends to map how the design process moves from moments where thinking and possibilities are as broad as possible to situations that are purposefully narrowed down and focused on specific objectives and activities.

This model is divided into two "diamonds", the former one representing the Problem Space and the latter diamond referring to the Solution Space. Each diamond is split into its halves, resulting in four distinct phases: Discover and Define (Problem Space), Develop and Deliver (Solution Space). The diamonds' shape represents the processes of exploring a problem (challenge, quest, project) more widely, resorting to divergent thinking, and then taking a much more focused action where thinking is expected to converge.

Here's how the Design Council introduces each of these four D moments:

- Discover. This stage helps people understand, rather than simply assume, what the problem is. The Discover stage involves speaking to and spending time with people who are affected by the issues to be addressed.
- Define. The insight gathered from the Discovery phase can help you to define the challenge in a different and clearer way.
- Develop. This phase encourages gathering different people to give answers to the clearly defined problem, seeking

inspiration from diverse sources and selecting ideas to be prototyped.
- Deliver. It involves testing out different solutions at small-scale, rejecting those that will not work and improving the ones that will and which can hopefully end up being implemented.

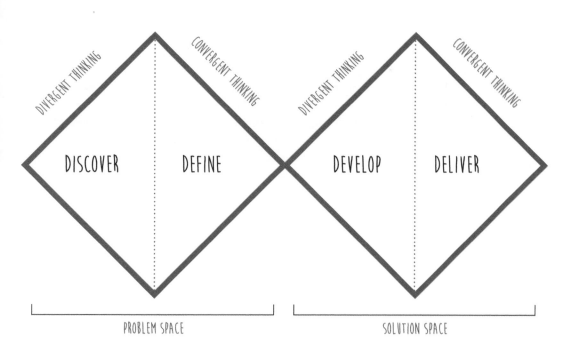

Interestingly, there are some similarities between the DD model and the monomyth, namely in regard to a match between their main moments. If we look at both frameworks backwards...

- **Deliver** is in great correspondence with **Give Back to Society**. This is when the hero initiates the road back to his/her Ordinary World with the Treasure or Elixir, after the adventure resulting in a positive outcome (i.e. the solution) that can be shared with others. The hero shows the benefit of his/her achievement, using it to heal a wound, or to accomplish tasks that had been unresolved in the Ordinary World. This is when, in the Double Diamond, you validate your solution and initiate a dissemination plan so your achievement can be adequately delivered.
- **Develop** is closely aligned with **Assemble a Team of Allies**. If, according to the Double Diamond, co-design and collaboration with multidisciplinary teams is welcome at this stage, one is expected to fight the barriers against creativity and identify possible solutions. Similarly, in the monomyth the hero resorts to allies and friends to face the problem, overcome the ordeal (and all the collateral crises) and finally find the Treasure.
- **Define** and **Discover** both correspond to **Growing from Adversities**. As we continue looking into these frameworks backwards, Define corresponds to the establishment of how the hero is to approach the challenge and the area to focus upon, while Discover, the first phase in the Double Diamond, corresponds to the stage in which the hero accepts the one challenge, breaking down its brief into smaller and researcheable bits.

The trouble is, as we've seen, the hero's journey starts way before he/she accepts the challenge or even before knowing which challenge he/she is supposed to take on — and only then Discover, Define, Develop and Deliver. So, what I'm saying is that, in the DD model, I can't find a match for when the hero initiates the journey — which is when they question the *status quo*, when they first receive the call to adventure (and that can be more than one), when they reject it, doubt it and examine it, looking at the call(s) from all possible future angles.

So, I suggest that there is a moment of pre-engagement with something that may become a project (or not), a moment which takes place before the first stage of the Double Diamond. This is a "zero moment of truth" to which I call **Determine** and which aligns with the **Going on a Journey** phase of the monomyth, where individuals or teams are still unable to Discover, since the step of choosing which project to go for is still to be taken.

Winning the Zero
Moment of Truth
https://www.
thinkwithgoogle.com

The Impact Plan introduces the need and awareness to such an important stage, where individuals would focus on identifying the possible levels of impact of each of those possible projects at a point when, undoubtedly, some decision-making is already taking place (if not for other reasons, because the exclusion of one or more projects is needed). Many of these early decisions will have critical implications during the remaining D stages. So, I call this preliminary phase *Determine* because this is when one *determines* which call/project to pick and commits to it with the right level of *determination*.

DETERMINE
CORRESPONDS TO
GOING ON A JOURNEY

I'm far from proposing that there is something like half a diamond missing to the DD model, because we know its focus on the processes around the one challenge are universal and have been widely tested. What I'm suggesting is that project thinking and mentorship can both start before the *jewellery* analogy, at a time when the individual (or team) either receives more than one call, or faces one call that seems to be tangential to his/her/their previously identified purpose. I'm indeed suggesting that anticipating and assessing the possible impact of one or more calls to adventure happens before discovering what's actually in the adventure. And perhaps I'm also saying

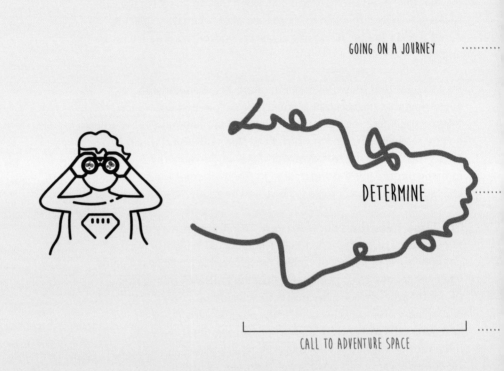

GOING ON A JOURNEY · · · · · · · · · ·

DETERMINE · · · · · · · ·

CALL TO ADVENTURE SPACE · · · · · · ·

that *sensitivity to initial conditions* is not exclusive to the hard sciences; it may be something to consider as well in the context of human and social knowledge and practice, which is where design best sits.

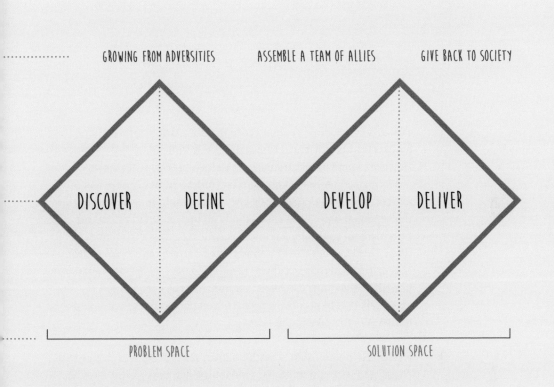

GROWING FROM ADVERSITIES   ASSEMBLE A TEAM OF ALLIES   GIVE BACK TO SOCIETY

DISCOVER   DEFINE   DEVELOP   DELIVER

PROBLEM SPACE   SOLUTION SPACE

Anticipating future possibilities

Edward Norton Lorenz was born in 1917 in West Hartford, Connecticut. He developed his fascination "by changes in the weather" since he was a little boy and completed his studies in mathematics with a master's degree from Harvard in 1940. During World War II he joined the Army Air Corps and trained as a weather forecaster at MIT, where he earned a doctorate in meteorology and worked until his death in 2008. By the late

1950s, he was using a computer to run simulations of weather models for his statistical forecasting techniques.

However, some of his simulations yielded precise patterns or repeating sequences which were far from what really happens in meteorology. When in the 60s one of his simulations deviated from the expected path, he realised that a change as small as the one he'd made in rounding a number can create a vast difference over time. This is where the aforementioned *butterfly effect* comes from. Lorenz realised that *sensitivity to initial conditions* is what causes non periodic behaviour; the more a system has the capacity to vary, the less likely it is to produce a repeating, expected sequence — and the harder it is to make predictions.

Nassim Nicholas Taleb, a mathematical statistician and risk analyst concerned with randomness, probability, and uncertainty says that forecasting the future is nearly impossible since what we know is much smaller in relation to what we do not know, adding that human beings are programmed to learn specific things and not to think about generalities. The truth is that since the very beginnings, humans have been enchanted with the idea of knowing the future.

For over 5000 years the I-Ching, which can be understood both as an oracle and a book of wisdom, has been used and relied on by millions of people to aid in decision making and predicting the future. The answers or predictions of events are revealed by using a numerological system based on the Yin and Yang, where the Yin is represented by a broken line and the Yang by a whole line. A combination of lines leads to figures usually formed by six lines (the hexagrams) which later resulted in a deck of 64 cards,

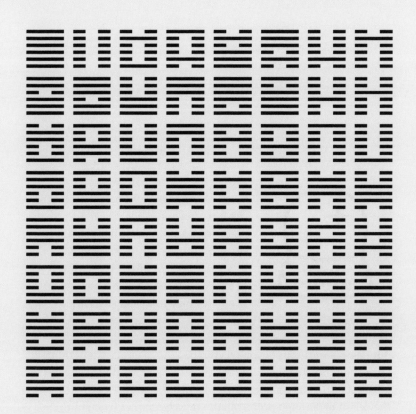

King Wen's Sequence of Hexagrams
I Ching or Book of Changes: Ancient Chinese wisdom to inspire and enlighten

each one expressing an archetypical truth. Its semiotic complexity makes the I-Ching one of the most elaborate systems of divination and meaning that ever existed. Much later, in western cultures, cartomancy became a popular method of divination. Tarot decks are known to have been used to gain insight into future events since around 1750, being the Tarocco Bolognese one of its early versions.

Recently, and much less mystical, an example of fortune telling is the Magic 8-Ball, a toy commercialised by Mattel, the basic principle of which is a random answer out of 20 different options: the user asks a yes-no question, turns the ball over and gets an answer which is displayed on the ball's screen (the possibilities are ten affirmative, five non-committal, and five negative answers). I should also mention Paul II, the octopus who, in 2010, correctly predicted the outcomes of eight World Cup matches played by the German team...

Tea leaves, crystal balls, spots on the livers of animals, flight patterns of birds, the lines in your hands, are all techniques and resources that have been useful to the powers of prophecy and divinatory arts, resorting to the interpretation of signs, fantastic objects, and hidden geometry for the advanced notice of omens.

But fear me not! This is not exactly the kind of anticipatory thinking I want to promote in you. In fact, there are slightly different ways for us to establish connections with the future, not necessarily through the occult or through probabilistic ways, but rather by building scenarios — plausible fictions about what might or could happen.

There's always been visionaries creating fictionalised narratives in which the most fantastic and unimaginable things happen in some moment in the future — people like Alvin Toffler, Aldous Huxley, Buckminster Fuller, Jules Verne, among many others. Things that quite often turn out to become true a few decades later. Also, museums used to be those places where we could find collections of evidence of our past and current times, but museology has evolved into showcasing scenarios of a time that lies ahead of us. Two excellent examples are The Museum of Tomorrow (Museu do Amanhã) in Rio de Janeiro, and The Museum of the Future in Dubai, both inviting us to discover and imagine the future. The latter guides visitors through a journey to 2071, from which we should return more open to new possibilities to shape today's world for the better.

Museum of Tomorrow
https://museudoamanha.org.br

Museum of the Future
https://museumofthefuture.ae/en

On his book Wanderful, David Pearl tells us about an agency called A Hundred Years (100yea.rs), which filters its clients based on their

David Pearl
*Wanderful: Human
navigation for a complex
world*

willingness to think a century ahead, grounded on the argument that such a long-time frame, one in which people have to imagine a world in which they no longer exist, shifts their perspective into questioning their purpose here and now. Less ambitious timewise, but following the same principle, Milton Glaser used to ask his design students to write a detailed place description of their perfect day at work five years in the future. Basically, the design legend was asking his students to speculate on a destination, a vision to hold on to, one that would help them in orienting their studies and define their career goals.

Speculative Design, also known as Design Fiction, took form in the early 90s as a response by designers who were frustrated by serving a mass-market machine, which led them to question their role in consumerism and its impact on the planet. They were captive of the *form follows function* and *form follows emotion* ways of thinking and making.

Coined at the beginning of the 20th century by American architect Louis Henry Sullivan, the *form follows function* maxim defended that the best possible form results from the intended function. Later in the 80s, designer Hartmut Esslinger, founder of frogdesign, proposed that *form follows emotion*, since he wanted design to be fuelled by sensuality and emotions, thereby facilitating people's access to technical products — but it brought issues about programmed obsolescence, for example, ending to be seen as a motto not sufficiently concerned with a better world. Speculation in design asks us to zoom out and to think what the effects of designs on future societies can be. It doesn't try to predict the future. It concerns possibilities, not probabilities. It pushes us to consider preferences and needs over a set of possible scenarios, spurring new ideas toward a preferable and sustainable future.

BTW, if you need a break, this may be a good time for you to watch *Interstellar*.

Notes, thoughts, drawings, ideas ...
When you're done with your break, take a moment to reflect on what
you just went through over this short journey (i.e. half a chapter). What
can you anticipate about the future?

Form follows purpose

The timescales for scenario creation can vary from a few months to many decades ahead. Scenarios are not meant to be predictions of the future, they are a means to project likely future circumstances, in order to reflect on these and to inform action to be taken.

This is what **The Impact Plan** does. It is not a game of chance, and its cards are not randomly picked to offer you an accidental answer. Instead, it provides users with guidance towards self-awareness and sensitivity to initial conditions, supporting the definition of a purpose and setting up the territory for short-term scenarios to surface. In parallel, it supports the construction or revision of mid-term career intentions, in a way helping users build their agency and authority in finding meaningful solutions for real-world problems of their concern (even if future, long-term ones).

The Impact Plan is a reflexivity-led resource that sets the ground for the speculation of impact and prepares us as humanity-centred individuals. We do that by looking into the broader landscape with the sustainability binoculars and a transformational attitude, developing greater awareness of the contexts we live in and proceed to adjust career ambitions to find our place in a vertiginously changing world. **The Impact Plan** establishes that *form follows purpose*.

Several visual canvases or board-like tools have been created and developed in the last few years, mostly to support innovation, development, and design thinking. The problem identified is that none establishes the link between purpose-led reflexivity and speculation at the different levels of possible impact. None is there to support the Determine stage, in which intuitive and less disciplined scenarios inspired by a *sensitivity to initial conditions* are essential for the anticipation of what may be a preferable good life in the future. Our interest in the future is permanent and it is perfectly human since the future represents the dimension in which our ambitions and investments take place. The future means the unknown — which is where we are all heading to. Exciting, right?

In their book, Ian Alexander, independent consultant specialising in requirements engineering, and Neil Maiden, Professor of Digital Creativity at City, University of London, say it all: "scenarios are a powerful antidote to the complexity of systems". Because scenarios resort to storytelling — an activity we all know too well since very early years — they provide us with a holistic view of a certain situation/goal (through text, graphics, images and prototypes), which is depicted through a sequence of actions (as in a story), allowing us to quickly identify vulnerabilities, disparities and exclusions. There are several approaches for the creation of scenarios, namely the Evolution Case, the Alternative Case, the Exception Case, and the What-If scenario. Any of these make us engage with the future through storytelling. Just not the kind of story that begins with Once Upon a Time but the one that starts with Sometime in the Future...

Ian F. Alexander & Neil Maiden
Scenarios, Stories, Use Cases: Through the Systems Development Life-Cycle

Sometime in the Future

How about you giving it a try in speculation? Create a short fiction for each one of the scenarios in this exercise. Start with the simpler one below, and then move to the next page to discover your speculative capabilities. Each story is about the same character (which is YOU) who wishes to make the world a better place. You may want to consider Political, Economic, Social, Technological, Legal and Environmental factors and/or trends, but also your own personal circumstances, both known and unknown.

EVOLUTION CASE

All trends continue as expected. Things gently move toward achieving the expected goal. It's just a matter of time.

60 mn

The Rolling Stones
Fortune Teller

ALTERNATIVE CASE	EXCEPTION CASE	WHAT-IF
A more or less static picture of an imagined future situation. Consider your assumptions and the usual meanings of things and question them, turning them upside down.	Also known as Negative Scenario, it describes an undesired event (an error, a pandemic, a war, an earthquake, your own flaws, etc.), an opposition by hostile agents that interferes with progress towards your goal. Play evil!	A scenario in which new, disruptive factors (positive or negative) fundamentally change the situation. What if your life becomes totally dysfunctional? What if you win the lottery? What if you are abducted by aliens?

Speculative (heroic) scenarios

As Professor of Design Theory Anne-Marie Willis says, it is certainly difficult to make connections between large scale forces – climate, economics, societal change – and the mundane details of our everyday life. I agree with her in that many of us turn our back on the problems we know exist just because "You Only Live Once" (YOLO) — and due to that people decide not to spend too much time preoccupied with what is still to come. It is an attitude that only either alienated conscientious objectors or the complete ignorant can afford to have.

Anne-Marie Willis
Designing Back from the Future

A member of the Faculty of Applied Sciences and Arts, at the German University in Cairo, Dr Willis distinguishes between large-scale and small-scale scenarios, and between reactive and proactive ones. Large-scale are usually long-term scenarios that narrate things decades ahead, projecting in the future — in a generalised manner — the current and known trends that affect society globally. On the other hand, small-scale tend to be short-term specific scenarios, focused on a particular solution thought for a particular beneficiary. Reactive scenarios are concerned with "what might happen", in a preparation of answers to what may affect our known and traditional circumstances. Trends and existing data over-determine these narratives in order to create distinctive and credible stories about the future, supporting the identification of opportunities that inform strategy and decision-making. Finally, proactive scenarios are concerned with "what might be possible". These are created by asking questions that make us think on how the future circumstances could differ from those we know, making room for challenging our notions of everydayness; however, Dr Willis suggests scenarios must be used both in creative and informed ways, since they can quickly be corrupted by unhelpful utopian thinking.

In fact, what **The Impact Plan** aims at is supporting the creation of *protopian futures* — not utopian (imaginary, perfect and ideal) or dystopian (imaginary, undesirable, usually catastrophic) ones. The term *protopia* was proposed by futurist thinker and editor of Wired magazine, Kevin Kelly, to represent a narrative of a future that can be created from constant and continuous improvements, and which depends on both personal and community effort. Protopia is a preferable non idealistic state that is better than yesterday and today — although it may be only just a little bit better.

Peter Schwartz
The Art of the Long View:
Planning for the Future in an
Uncertain World

Trevor Hancock &
Clement Bezold
Possible futures, preferable
futures

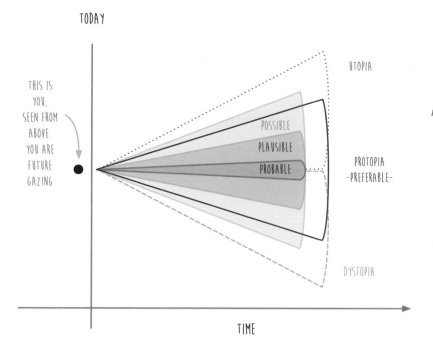

Protopian Futures

Define a timeframe. Think of you in each of the quadrants on the next page considering the following:

- Small-scale scenarios are focused on a particular solution thought for a particular beneficiary, hence considering a specific user or local community and their needed products, services, events, or application of technology.
- Large-scale scenarios contemplate known trends that affect society globally such as climate conditions and resource availability, social advancements and constraints, technology developments and backlashes, economic and political circumstances.
- Reactive scenarios provide credible answers to what may affect your known circumstances for which you want to consider demographic trends, consumer trends, possible economic and political events, climate-change factors, resource availability, technological developments.
- Proactive scenarios imply thinking on how the future circumstances could differ from those we know, going beyond demographic, social, economic, climatic, political, technological trends.

Now, let's try and get some answers:

- How would you distribute your four scenarios between today and the future?
- What quadrants would suit them best?
- How could large scale forces play out in small scale contexts?

30 mn

The National
About Today

Stereophonics
Maybe Tomorrow

PROACTIVE

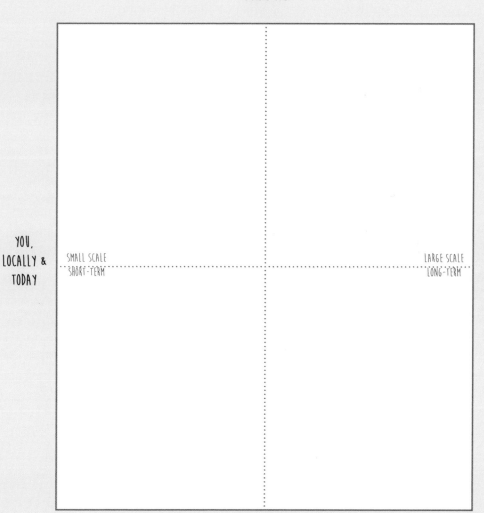

YOU,
LOCALLY &
TODAY

SMALL SCALE
SHORT-TERM

LARGE SCALE
LONG-TERM

YOU,
GLOBALLY
& IN THE
FUTURE

REACTIVE

Forecasting, Backcasting

Looking at the future makes us look at today differently and the greatest advantage of scenarios is that they invite us to take a backward glance until our time travel reaches today.

Future Timeline
https://www.futuretimeline.net

So, we know now the process begins with some forecasting, by setting a goal and projecting existing prognosis, past and current trends, and expected behaviours forward in time. You won't have to struggle to find these as you'll get dozens of relevant results with a simple Internet search. Once you're happy and with sufficient material to back you up, define a specific place and time (which need to be relevant to the parties involved) for each of your scenarios. You may want to have more than one scenario and none necessarily pointing towards the same moment in the future. Rather, you may wish to speculate on them sequentially.
Characters, settings and events are imagined – in the form of written narratives, role-plays, prototypes. A plausible narrative is created carrying a clear goal that must, by all means, be achieved.

So, say you are now 50 years ahead in time, thanks to the previous scenario-creation activities. You have travelled to the future, envisioned a preferable situation for you and for all... but you can't stay there. You must now travel back and work on how your protopian answers can be implemented. Backcasting is this exercise through which, after defining one or multiple desired futures and timeframes, you look back to assess what would be required to get there.

At the Determine stage, you would assess which one of your Calls to Adventure is the most appropriate for you to move forward. Just start by asking questions (don't leave them with no answer):

- What call will you take on to avoid the exception case, negative scenario, should that be possible?
- Can you map step-by-step paths, back from worst-case scenarios, so you know which project or call to avoid?
- What needs to be designed – between now and the time of your preferable circumstance — to facilitate the positive scenarios you encountered?
- Is there any credible and valid alternative scenario that occurs through one of your calls that could unfold over time to get you there?

Retrospective thinking (also known as *retros*) occurs not only when you remember something from the past, but also when you think about hypothetical future scenarios to define how to move forward. Retros are an important part of the Determine stage because you start thinking about how the future you envisioned might be constructed and anticipated, moving backwards whilst constantly assessing your goals. So, this would be that moment when you reinvent the courses of action that will help you close the gap between the current state and your desired first outcome — which is to decide what project to pick.

There are several tools that help you in this process of moving back from the future, but we would highlight The Thing From The Future, an award-winning ideation card game that challenges players to articulate objects from alternative futures. The deck consists of 100+ cards that belong to four different categories — the type of future the "thing" comes from, the "thing's" thematic context, its basic form, and the emotion the "thing" generates in individuals from the present. Participants play their cards onto the table until they have a card from each category, which will allow them to ideate a creative concept. The other players vote on which concept is the best, the funniest, the most ironic, but the game gives you room to include other criteria, such as the most credible, the most creative, the most disruptive, the healthiest, the most environmentally friendly, etc.

The Thing from the Future
http://situationlab.org

Nevertheless, it is important to remind you that during these processes, as time passes by, both in travelling to the future and in travelling back to where we are today, requirements, needs and assumptions change. That means you'll have to reconcile and harmonise all your possible moves and actions during your homecoming, assessing the impact of any actions and assumptions your scenarios may involve. And that can be a tough, arduous job!

I see **The Impact Plan** as a reconciliation tool, gathering a set of prompts that guide you into this process of looking at what you do and how you do it, giving you an augmented sense of responsibility as you unfold a number of unforeseen implications. Anyway, backcasting requires not only analytical and research skills but, most of all, willingness to think outside the box, essential to *determining* the desired goal. **The Impact Plan** and any other tool are helpless if you're not sufficiently equipped with the competencies and motivation to get this done.

30 mn

LTJ Bukem
Horizons

Back from the Future

Distribute your scenarios around the oblique timeline. Remember that in backcasting your starting point is always the Future (1). By considering your Goal (2), check which scenarios are feasible and which ones need to be carefully thought through — since they may occur. As you move back to the present Now (3), circle the scenarios you feel will help you achieve your goal and strikethrough the ones that don't. Once you arrive, you should be ready to start planning (4) — and only then initiate the Discover stage of the Double Diamond framework.

PLAN

4

FUTURE

1

3

NOW

2

GOAL

Notes, thoughts, drawings, ideas ...

And now, reflect on what this other half of a chapter meant to you. Are there any tensions or inspiring prompts? Anything you'd like to further explore?

Assemble your Allies and
Achieve a Result

Heroes are made by the path they choose, not the powers they are graced with.
[Iron Man]

Currently, both academia and industry are being increasingly asked for clear contributions to the wicked, ugly problems that society faces. It seems relevant — if not obvious — to systematically enhance the idea of impact, guiding people through the selection of projects that best align to their existing and desired skillset, to their definition of a good life, to their entrepreneurial drive, and to their ambition towards making an impactful and meaningful addition to the world — even if just a tiny one. The cherry on top is that you can also plan for not spending a few miserable months working on a project that may lead to great outcomes and accomplishments, the carrying out or development of which means draining you from all the joy — either because you have a terrible relationship with the project leader, or because you have been picked up to be part of a team whose methods and tools you do not understand, or because it means long hours of meetings over the weekend, or simply because the team is distributed around the globe and the different time zones continuously compromise your family dinner. You can, in fact, anticipate some of these possibly nasty experiences and engage with the projects that will provide you with pleasurable moments.

So, I guess we've reached the moment where you are ready to acknowledge the following universal truth — the one that nobody else ever told you before:

YOU ARE ONLY AS GOOD A HERO AS YOUR PLAN FOR IMPACT

The next thing you need to know is the axiom deriving from it:

YOU WILL ONLY MAKE AN IMPACT IF YOU GET THE RIGHT SUPPORT TO GET YOUR RESULT RIGHT.

By support I mean whatever holds you up. It can come from those close to you that believe in your heroic intentions — such as *friends, family,* and *fools* too. You can also get support by equipping yourself of certain tools and resources that augment or optimise your skills and abilities. But you won't get much from your BFFFFs (Best Friends-Family-Fools Forever) or from your highly technological tools and state-of-the-art resources if you're not authentically

and consciously motivated. Being authentically and consciously motivated means you can tell the difference between the two voices that will be driving you: your gut emotions and feelings — telling you that what you feel is right — and your rational argument — which tells you that what you know is, most likely, the right thing to do in that given context, for that moment in time. Most importantly, despite being aware that the right thing may differ from what you feel is right, you are intrinsically motivated toward resolving a certain problem because you know its solution (even if just a portion of it) will have a positive impact both on you and on Humanity. All this to say that your most important ally is your own motivation. The one that makes your purpose sparkle, that convinces your BFFFFs, and brings about the best possible use of your tools and resources.

Now, I have no intention of competing with your BFFFFs but I believe I can help you by introducing you to this tool that will encourage you in answering the question "How can I (as a hero) anticipate the impact of my projects — and choose the most PLEASURABLE, MEANINGFUL, AND IMPACTFUL one?"

An ally that looks and feels like a boardgame

In a webinar promoted by the Design Management Institute in early 2021, designer Nick Munro said that the development of new generative and creative tools should only lead to better outcomes, by giving design, creativity, and innovation a fighting chance to shape the future, providing practical guidance to decision makers. Now, this is when modesty is set aside because I want to say that **The Impact Plan** fits just nicely here.

It is a tool that provides individuals with guidance towards self-awareness of the implications concerning each project or call to adventure (that may be under consideration). Also, the construction or redefinition of career intentions invading each of us, every now and then, may well be a way to help building the necessary agency and authority to find meaningful solutions for real-world problems. We know Design is a field inherently interdisciplinary, often focused on anticipating a future that does not yet exist, or on solving existing complex problems for multiple stakeholders. **The Impact Plan** sets the ground, firstly, for the speculation of impact, and finally, for the orientation toward a solution that will fully or partially solve an actual, existing problem. For that, you will engage in an informal speculative exercise about future scenarios, in which any project or challenge you may engage with will have implications on your future life and, ultimately, in the lives of many other. It is worth mentioning that the future starts somewhere around the next second...

The Impact Plan prepares you as a humanity-centred individual, looking into the broader landscape with a sustainability lens and a transformational attitude, developing greater awareness concerning the contexts we live in. And from there, you'll adjust your personal, communal, and professional ambitions, and find your ever-changing place in our dynamic and uncertain world.

As a tool, **The Impact Plan** includes the following three elements:

1. Two personas

When you anticipate the impact of your projects you will be looking into the interests of two kinds of entities, involved in and affected by both the design and execution process and the accomplished solution:

- *You, the Hero* (and/or your team) — those who are mostly and deeply concerned with the resolution of the problem underpinning the one challenge that will end up being selected for its highest impact. When I say the projects or interventions you get to be involved with must be pleasurable and meaningful, I mean there must be some objectives that are all about you having a great experience. When you anticipate impact concerning this persona, you do that by taking into account your self-interest "experience goals".

- *Humanity*, or if you want, all of us. Those around us and those far from us, our children, grandchildren, and the generations to come. The direct and indirect, broader beneficiaries, not always those the resolution of the problem targets, but those that ultimately benefit from it, should the identified outcome achieve such success that its implementation spreads beyond its initial and specific context. When you anticipate impact considering this persona, you do it by setting altruistic "life goals". Good life ones.

2. Three moments in the future

Impact will be anticipated considering three different moments in which you should look for some kind of value or reward:

- **Short-term**, *what's in it for me during the journey.*
  This value-moment focuses on the period starting the day you and/or your team identify the most impactful project to work on (basically, when you've completed the Determine stage), and until the day you hand it over to the "client" (which can be yourself). It is, basically, the timeframe of involvement in the design, development and implementation of the project, for which reason, when assessing more than one possible challenge, you and/or your team must anticipate the impact each of these will have on your life during such time. The final impact scores your projects will get, partially depend on your assessment on how each project will make you have a great time in researching, developing, testing and defending them. You don't want the selected project to be a months-long nightmare, you want it to be PLEASURABLE. So, your short-term scenarios must include an essential characteristic: enjoyment whilst learning. The impact of happily engaging with a certain new activity/project will be mainly on your own development as an individual, on your immediate wellbeing, on your small victories and rapid turnaround, on your motivation to develop new skills and willingness to put in practice the competences you have already acquired. That means your expectation (possibly not conscious) is to get some kind of more or less immediate reward or value inherent in the experience of performing certain activities

or engaging in a specific challenge: things like spending
more time with your friends, travel more, develop research
skills, become increasingly sharp and creative, complete
a degree, attend an event and get to interview (or simply
drink some tea with) someone really famous — these will be
the sort of short-term outcomes of your selected challenge.

- **Mid-term**, *what's in it for me once I find a solution.*
  Most of us have or dream with having a career. A minimally
  successful one that provides us with opportunities for
  the development of our capacities, the expansion of
  our networks and attainment of our ambitions. So, the
  culmination of a career is accomplishment — that's it. You
  don't want the selected project to keep you in the shadows
  or exactly where you are now, you want it to be MEANINGFUL.
  This value-moment is all about anticipating the impact
  each of the challenges or projects under consideration will
  have on your career intentions. Hence, it is a medium-term
  looking ahead, where you find an answer to a very specific
  question: *how will each of the challenges/projects contribute
  to the conditions and skills you need in order to follow the
  career path that best brings about your vocation?* The creation
  of such scenario will nudge you toward rethinking and
  rewinding your future plans and needs, contemplating your
  interests, preferences, passions and, simultaneously, how all
  these align to what really means solving the challenges you
  will face.

The previous two *moments in the future* are the self-centred time zones of **The Impact Plan** — mostly concerned with what's in it for the hero. The following moment is mostly interested in looking into what and who's around you besides you, i.e. persona Humanity.

- ***Long-term**, what's in it for Humanity.*
  This is the most benevolent and broad-minded scenario, driven by altruistic principles, the Others, and the planet, with sustainability at its core. This value-moment is expected to occur when the solution (to be found for the project you'll be working on) is already spreading and bringing positive contributions to the beneficiaries. This is more likely to happen if you anticipate how your performance and engagement with a project can lead to a concrete solution that is of value not just to you, but also to a larger number of individuals, ranging from your neighbours next door, local communities, or industry sectors to international causes. This is where I like to speak of Triple I (3I) Impact: it's got to be International, Interdisciplinary and Intersectoral. You don't want the selected project to remain a vanity (for yourself and/or your client), with limited range in its application — you want it to be IMPACTFUL. This kind of scenario is usually inspired by higher-level altruistic motivations, where the reward is related to assisting the resolution of a wider problem, ultimately leading to a sense of fulfilment. To anticipate this value-moment, you are in Humanity-centred thinking mode, pondering the impact of truly being a hero.

3. Five contexts of impact

To guide you during this complex journey of speculation, **The Impact Plan** has been broken down into five different and colourful contexts: two of them dedicated to persona You, the Hero — *Learning* and *Career*, both focused on your Development and Wellbeing — and the remaining three for the foretelling around persona Humanity — grounded on the three dimensions of sustainability: *Economic*, *Environmental* and *Social*.

Summing up:

PERSONAS	VALUE-MOMENT	CONTEXT OF IMPACT
You, the Hero	Short-term	Learning
	Mid-term	Career
Humanity	Long-term	Economic
		Environmental
		Social

Finally, **The Impact Plan** is operationalised by resorting to two boardgame-like components:

- a deck of outcome cards, organised after the five colourful contexts of impact and kinds of reward, making you reflect on very specific (and possible) outcomes,
- a one-page canvas or, as an alternative and which you'll find on this book, a group of boards for you to map out your identified forms of impact.

IMPACT ON...	CONTEXT	REWARD	SPECIFIC OUTCOMES
You, the Hero	Learning	Development	Effective Communication Information Literacy Problem Solving Strategic Thinking Creativity Ethical/Moral Awareness Pluridisciplinarity
		Wellbeing	Expenses & Risks Loved Ones & Privacy Personal Activities
	Career	Development	Influence & Legitimacy Change in Career Path Entrepreneurship Promotion & Salary
		Wellbeing	Self & Loved Ones
Humanity	Economic		Developed Models
	Environmental		Planet & Species
	Social		Advanced Society Universal Communities

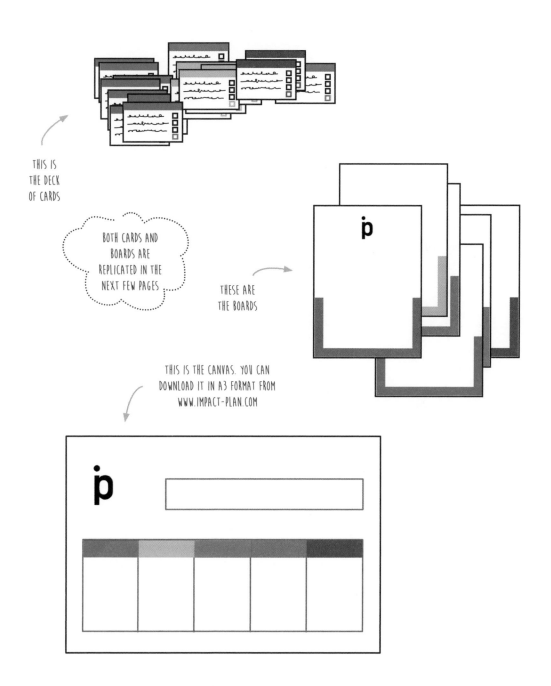

THIS IS
THE DECK
OF CARDS

BOTH CARDS AND
BOARDS ARE
REPLICATED IN THE
NEXT FEW PAGES

THESE ARE
THE BOARDS

THIS IS THE CANVAS. YOU CAN
DOWNLOAD IT IN A3 FORMAT FROM
WWW.IMPACT-PLAN.COM

The cards include several prompts (the stimuli) for speculation around possible outcomes and for rationale-led narratives to emerge — which help to convince yourself, your team (if applicable), your clients, supervisors, and managers that project X is the right one for now.

The cards' stimuli provide you with contextual possibilities to assess the impact you anticipate for each project (let's call them Project 1, Project 2, and Project 3), using a scale ranging from -2 (for very negative impact) to +2 (for very positive impact). Each card will produce an impact score per project which you get by adding the scores of all stimuli from that card.

You use the boards or the canvas to define each of your to-be-assessed projects and their beneficiaries, and also to register the quantitative final impact scores of each project under consideration. Once you have decided which project you will be working on (because of its expected higher impact), you will also use the boards or canvas to get a holistic view of your five impact contexts, their most relevant stimuli (hopefully lots of +2s, but without losing sight of the -2s that may compromise some of the expected outcomes), and how each stimulus relates to the others, within and across contexts.

There is no specific order on how the canvas/boards and cards ought to be used. You can start by anticipating the impact each project will have on persona *You, the hero* and, as you progress throughout the value-moments and contexts, use those initial outcomes as causes that may lead to certain larger scale (humanitarian) effects. Or, you can start with persona *Humanity* living in a preferred world, and move backwards, unwrapping the possible future achievements to find out what you might have done or invested in and that might contribute to such impact. Ultimately, both boards/canvas and cards are meant to be scoring devices to back you up in choosing the most impactful and personally relevant project/activity/challenge. And I really want to stress out that, despite thought in a timeline kind of way, **The Impact Plan** can be used either linearly or in a non-sequential manner. If you choose the boards rather than the canvas, you can display them in any order you wish. You can even change their order — to look at things from a different and sometimes unpredictable angle.

You should now give it a try. You can either use the next few pages (which contain all the boards and cards), or you can download the canvas or the boards, whilst requesting access to the cards from www.impact-plan.com.

And I promise, shortly after that you'll get an answer from me!

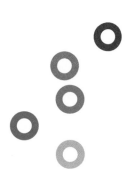

The rules of the ally

As in any alliance, to get the best out of **The Impact Plan** there are some (but not many) established ways one must observe. There are basically 10 steps, split through three main recommendations:

1. *State your possible heroic challenges and find their beneficiaries.*
   STEP 1 | STEP 2

2. *Play the cards and do the (easy-peasy) maths.*
   STEP 3 | STEP 4 | STEP 5 | STEP 6

3. *Pick the most impactful challenge and find the hidden gems of impact.*

State your possible heroic challenges and find their beneficiaries

STEP 1

Use the Gauge board on page 90 (or the top section of the canvas) to define up to three project/activity topics currently under consideration. You can do that by using:

- a title-like sentence (e.g. *the importance of leguminous grains in children's nutrition*), or
- a goal-oriented statement (*to communicate the nutritious importance of leguminous grains to children*), or
- a guiding question (*how might we better communicate the nutritious importance of leguminous grains to children?*).

I recommend the latter, namely for team-based projects, because thinking in a "How Might We" kind of way heavily relies on abductive logic, which is seen as the starting point of a research process, acknowledging the uncertainty of data.

Michael Gottlieb, Emilie Wagner, Alexei Wagner & Teresa Chan
Applying Design Thinking Principles to Curricular Development in Medical Education

The "how" assumes that there is a solution. "Might" assures it is acceptable whether an idea works or not. "We" emphasizes collaboration. The prompt works as a source of inspiration for idea generation that broadens perspectives, discovers connections, and generates unexpected ideas.

Abduction starts with an observation leading to an inference to the best explanation to the problem, i.e., the simplest and most likely conclusion from the observation. Although our observation may not leave us certain, abductive thinking serves to orient us in our surroundings. And we've seen before that there is nothing usual or acquainted in the future; we make previsions based on what we know, based on data that's been gathered or produced today or the day before. Never tomorrow. Despite the many possible explanations for anything that we come across, we tend to abduce a single explanation in the expectation that we can better orient ourselves in our surroundings and disregard some possibilities. Remember — we're lazy. Potentially a nice bunch of heroes, but surely super lazy.

STEP 2

Once you have a sentence for each of the challenges you want to assess, it becomes easier to identify their main beneficiaries (one per challenge). A beneficiary is a person who benefits or derives advantage from something. In this case, this person benefits from you finding a solution to a problem that affects them, whether they are aware of it or not.

For the example challenge suggested before, the beneficiary would be in generic terms "children" — they would derive advantage from increasing consumption of grain legumes, which are high in protein, iron, zinc, folate and calcium. These grains also fend off malnutrition in food-deficit regions and help with controlling and reducing diet-related diseases, such as obesity and diabetes, in food surplus regions. You can specify who these children are and where they live to complete a one-sentence profile of your beneficiary (rather than just a word). If you got a client brief, this kind of demographic-related information is probably there. So you could come up with something like "Sicilian children in primary school" — where the client submitting such challenge is, say, the Regional Government of Sicily, in Italy.

Finally, don't worry about the score box; you'll return to this board (or to this part of the canvas) at a later stage.

The Gauge Board

15 mn

**Brooklyn Funk
Essentials**
*The Creator has a
Master Plan*

ṗ THE IMPACT PLAN

Completed by: _____   Date: _____

Project 1:

_____

_____

Beneficiary: Score: [ ]

_____

Project 2:

_____

_____

Beneficiary: Score: [ ]

_____

Project 3:

_____

_____

Beneficiary: Score: [ ]

_____

Play the cards and do the (easy-peasy) maths

STEP 3

The cards (pages 93-104) really are the core of **The Impact Plan** since they act as triggers for your thinking. The deck includes 19 (well... maybe 20...) Impact Cards representing the five impact contexts. You can use them all or just some of them. You may find that one or two are irrelevant in a given context, or that they simply do not align to one of your challenges (or personal needs). What really matters is that you appraise how the outcome promoted by each card (the outcome is, roughly, each card's title) can affect or influence the most each of your projects. In the next few pages you will find 10 cards for Learning, five for Career, one for Economic, one for Environmental and two for Social.

As said before, each card includes a list of stimuli (in some cards you can add your extra stimuli too!) that will help you in assessing the possible impact of each project. And for that, there are two pathways:

- you can either focus on each stimulus and score it against each of your projects (using the 1, 2 and 3 boxes on the right simultaneously), or
- you can focus on each project at a time (say you start with Project 1) and run over the stimuli of each card, scoring these against the particularities of such project. In this case, you will have to revisit the cards again to assess Project 2 and then Project 3, if applicable.

Let's now have a deep look into each of the impact contexts, starting with those concerned with persona *You, the Hero*.

The Learning context anticipates the rewards and outcomes that you'll get for accepting and getting your hands on in a project. Its name derives from the fact that, regardless of your experience, profession or inflated ego, every project, challenge, or activity you get yourself involved with represents a source of new understanding, knowledge, behaviour, skills, values, attitudes, desires, and preferences. Basically, if you don't see yourself as a learner-for-life, you may want to think in a circular and sustainable way of getting rid of this book.

As a learner, there are two kinds of rewards you aim for:

- *Development*, because you want the new understanding, knowledge, behaviour, skills, values, attitudes, desires, and preferences to make you develop as an individual. This means you'll be interested in optimising your interactions with the others by developing your communication skills and your ethical and moral awareness, but you'll also be interested in approaching your projects in the most appropriate way, by developing your information literacy, your understanding of pluridisciplinarity, evolving in both your creative and strategic thinking and your problem-solving skills.

- *Wellbeing,* because if you're not well you won't attain any of the above. Hence, you want to guarantee all the good stuff that you need to keep a smile on your face whilst the duration of the project: health, safety, love and, of course, some money.

The Learning Cards

LEARNING > WELLBEING > PERSONAL ACTIVITIES *   1   2   3

- Practicing physical activity .... ☐☐☐
- Dedicating time to hobbies .... ☐☐☐
- Cleaning the house .... ☐☐☐
- Volunteering to causes .... ☐☐☐
- Following group commitments (religious, scouts, associations) ☐☐☐
- Reading or solving quizes/puzzles .... ☐☐☐
- Watching films/series/tv .... ☐☐☐
- Attending events (shows, gigs, exhibitions, etc.) .... ☐☐☐
- Changing established habits/vices .... ☐☐☐
- _____ .... ☐☐☐
- _____ .... ☐☐☐
- _____ .... ☐☐☐

* LESS TIME FOR IMPORTANT/MEANINGFUL ACTIVITIES SHOULD BE MARKED WITH LOWER IMPACT SCORES   ☐☐☐

LEARNING > WELLBEING > EXPENSES & RISKS *   1   2   3

- Attending complementary workshops or training .... ☐☐☐
- Travelling to collect data or present results .... ☐☐☐
- Purchasing equipment and/or materials .... ☐☐☐
- Issuing an insurance .... ☐☐☐
- Paying for space allocation (exhibitions, focus groups, etc.) ...... ☐☐☐
- Paying honoraries to third parties involved .... ☐☐☐
- Exposing to geographically unstable regions .... ☐☐☐
- Interacting with disturbed/violent individuals .... ☐☐☐
- Obtaining accredited documents or clearance .... ☐☐☐
- _____ .... ☐☐☐
- _____ .... ☐☐☐
- _____ .... ☐☐☐

* HIGHER COSTS AND RISKS SHOULD BE MARKED WITH LOWER IMPACT SCORES   ☐☐☐

LEARNING > WELLBEING > LOVED ONES & PRIVACY *

	1	2	3
- Meeting up with friends	☐	☐	☐
- Spending time with my family/partner	☐	☐	☐
- Eating healthily and regularly	☐	☐	☐
- Sleeping properly	☐	☐	☐
- Taking time to relax and deep breathing	☐	☐	☐
- Looking after myself (e.g. health check-up, massage, etc.)	☐	☐	☐
- _____	☐	☐	☐
- _____	☐	☐	☐
- _____	☐	☐	☐
- _____	☐	☐	☐
- _____	☐	☐	☐
- _____	☐	☐	☐

* LESS TIME FOR IMPORTANT/MEANINGFUL ACTIVITIES SHOULD BE MARKED WITH LOWER IMPACT SCORES

☐ ☐ ☐

LEARNING > DEVELOPMENT > EFFECTIVE COMMUNICATION

	1	2	3
- Improving active listening skills	☐	☐	☐
- Consistently interpreting and using non-verbal communication	☐	☐	☐
- Articulating follow-up questions	☐	☐	☐
- Creating concise verbal and visual messages	☐	☐	☐
- Adapting the tone of voice to the audience	☐	☐	☐
- Selecting/adapting means of comm. according to the context	☐	☐	☐
- Defining and developing a personal brand	☐	☐	☐
- Understanding accessibility and usability	☐	☐	☐
- Recognising the boundaries of digital social isolation	☐	☐	☐
- _____	☐	☐	☐
- _____	☐	☐	☐
- _____	☐	☐	☐

☐ ☐ ☐

LEARNING > DEVELOPMENT > ETHICAL & MORAL AWARENESS

	1	2	3
- Identifying ethical and moral dilemmas	☐	☐	☐
- Understanding and assessing ethical values and principles	☐	☐	☐
- Examining the implications of acts for the lives of others	☐	☐	☐
- Understanding deontology, authenticity and transparency	☐	☐	☐
- Assessing information obtained from different sources	☐	☐	☐
- Familiarising with diversity, inclusivity and equality	☐	☐	☐
- Recognising biases (conscious and unconscious)	☐	☐	☐
- _____	☐	☐	☐
- _____	☐	☐	☐
- _____	☐	☐	☐
- _____	☐	☐	☐
- _____	☐	☐	☐

☐ ☐ ☐

LEARNING > DEVELOPMENT > INFORMATION LITERACY   1   2   3

- Recognising and articulating a need for information .... ☐ ☐ ☐
- Distinguishing ways in which said need may be addressed .... ☐ ☐ ☐
- Constructing strategies for locating information .... ☐ ☐ ☐
- Locating and accessing information .... ☐ ☐ ☐
- Assessing information obtained from different sources .... ☐ ☐ ☐
- Using information appropriately and ethicaly .... ☐ ☐ ☐
- Creating usable information from raw data .... ☐ ☐ ☐
- Understanding multisensory perceptions of information .... ☐ ☐ ☐
- Publishing (e.g. blogging, directing) relevant information .... ☐ ☐ ☐
- Categorising and analysing information .... ☐ ☐ ☐
- Understanding the basics of digital data compliance .... ☐ ☐ ☐
- _____ .... ☐ ☐ ☐

       ☐ ☐ ☐

LEARNING > DEVELOPMENT > PROBLEM SOLVING   1   2   3

- Understanding complexity .... ☐ ☐ ☐
- Developing imagination and empathy .... ☐ ☐ ☐
- Generating alternatives and scenarios .... ☐ ☐ ☐
- Getting to know decision-making processes/tools .... ☐ ☐ ☐
- Developing project management skills .... ☐ ☐ ☐
- Understanding and implementing Design Thinking .... ☐ ☐ ☐
- Develop research skills .... ☐ ☐ ☐
- Improving analytical thinking .... ☐ ☐ ☐
- Developing my leadership potential .... ☐ ☐ ☐
- Engaging with non-routine situations .... ☐ ☐ ☐
- _____ .... ☐ ☐ ☐
- _____ .... ☐ ☐ ☐

       ☐ ☐ ☐

LEARNING > DEVELOPMENT > STRATEGIC THINKING   1   2   3

- Prioritising tasks .... ☐ ☐ ☐
- Being aware of biases .... ☐ ☐ ☐
- Identifying risks .... ☐ ☐ ☐
- Defining syrnergies .... ☐ ☐ ☐
- Improving listening skills .... ☐ ☐ ☐
- Refining questioning skills .... ☐ ☐ ☐
- Understanding causality and consequenciality .... ☐ ☐ ☐
- Understanding group dynamics .... ☐ ☐ ☐
- Defining pragmatic and realistic objectives .... ☐ ☐ ☐
- Identifying contexts and ecosystems .... ☐ ☐ ☐
- _____ .... ☐ ☐ ☐
- _____ .... ☐ ☐ ☐

       ☐ ☐ ☐

LEARNING > DEVELOPMENT > CREATIVITY

1 2 3

- Building confidence in my ideas .... ☐☐☐
- Overcoming negativism .... ☐☐☐
- Realising that most problems have multiple solutions .... ☐☐☐
- Understanding stereotypes and mental blocks .... ☐☐☐
- Engaging with sensorial representations of information .... ☐☐☐
- Looking for sources of inspiration .... ☐☐☐
- Developing imagination and desire .... ☐☐☐
- Speculating and creating alternative, unusual scenarios .... ☐☐☐
- Developing cultural awareness .... ☐☐☐
- Fighting the "Not-Invented-Here" syndrome .... ☐☐☐
- Questioning the status quo and changing things .... ☐☐☐
- Prototyping, trying, making .... ☐☐☐

☐☐☐

LEARNING > DEVELOPMENT > PLURIDISCIPLINARITY

1 2 3

- Identifying adjacent/different relevant disciplines .... ☐☐☐
- Identifying real-world complex issues .... ☐☐☐
- Understanding approaches systematically and holistically .... ☐☐☐
- Realising the contribution of different domains to the same issue ☐☐☐
- Engaging with flexible/innovative methods and practices .... ☐☐☐
- Coordinating and collaborating with others .... ☐☐☐
- Refining negotiation and persuasion skills .... ☐☐☐
- Understanding the boundaries of different domains .... ☐☐☐
- Creating comprehensive research questions .... ☐☐☐
- Developing concensual definitions and guidelines .... ☐☐☐
- Developing a global awareness .... ☐☐☐
- _____ .... ☐☐☐

☐☐☐

LEARNING > DEVELOPMENT > DIGITAL LITERACY

1 2 3

- Understanding the basics of accessibility and usability .... ☐☐☐
- Recognising the boundaries of digital social isolation .... ☐☐☐
- Complying with cibersecurity and e-safety .... ☐☐☐
- Distinguishing the implications of shared information .... ☐☐☐
- Understanding synchronous and asynchronous comms .... ☐☐☐
- Engaging with the basics of programming/coding .... ☐☐☐
- Filming, editing, podcasting, directing .... ☐☐☐
- Creating digital contents and publishing online and offline ...... ☐☐☐
- Implementing good practices of moderation or validation .... ☐☐☐
- Uploading, downloading, transferring contents .... ☐☐☐
- Performing advanced/boolean searches .... ☐☐☐
- Categorising, geolocating, tagging information .... ☐☐☐

☐☐☐

- BONUS
- CARD!

BECAUSE
ALL HEROES
NAVIGATE
THE DIGITAL
WORLD THESE
DAYS!

The Career context anticipates the professional rewards and outcomes to which you'll access at the end of your project's journey. Whether you are an established practitioner in your industry, or a student still juggling the indecision around all your different vocations, you'll want to use at least one of the cards of this context.

And just as in the previous impact context (Learning), in this one there are also the same two kinds of rewards:

- *Development*, because you want to move forward and get a chance to better your professional life. This means you may be interested in changing your career, choosing a slightly or very different path, or you may wish to become an authority and credible expert in a certain field, or simply look for the evidence that will help you to be promoted and negotiate increased perks, or you may want to call it a day and set up your own business, even if that means that, for a while, you won't get any salary at all.

- *Wellbeing*, because, again, if you're not in good shape, physically and mentally, there's no point in any of the above. This is to say that you want to keep that smile on your face after the project is over.

The Career Cards

CAREER > WELLBEING > SELF & LOVED ONES *	1	2	3
- Spending time with the meaningful/loved ones	☐	☐	☐
- Eating healthily and regularly	☐	☐	☐
- Commuting to and from work	☐	☐	☐
- Sleeping properly	☐	☐	☐
- Taking time to relax	☐	☐	☐
- Practising physical activity	☐	☐	☐
- Dedicating time to hobbies and social/cultural commitments	☐	☐	☐
- Reading and watching TV/series/Films	☐	☐	☐
- Attending events (cultural, entertainment, professional)	☐	☐	☐
- Changing established habits/vices	☐	☐	☐
- _____	☐	☐	☐
- _____	☐	☐	☐

* LESS TIME FOR IMPORTANT/MEANINGFUL ACTIVITIES SHOULD BE MARKED WITH LOWER IMPACT SCORES

| | ☐ | ☐ | ☐ |

CAREER > DEVELOPMENT > INFLUENCE & LEGITIMACY	1	2	3
- Building connections and hubs	☐	☐	☐
- Learning to listen	☐	☐	☐
- Learning persuasion techniques	☐	☐	☐
- Developing expertise and know-how	☐	☐	☐
- Mapping power structures	☐	☐	☐
- Getting to know stakeholders' needs, perspectives and interests	☐	☐	☐
- Developing leadership competencies	☐	☐	☐
- Understanding honesty and authenticity	☐	☐	☐
- Developing accountability for others	☐	☐	☐
- Developing emotional intelligence	☐	☐	☐
- Cultivate co-operative and collaborative working habits	☐	☐	☐
- Defining decision-making processes	☐	☐	☐

| | ☐ | ☐ | ☐ |

- Evaluating/questioning current job satisfaction .... ☐ ☐ ☐
- Assessing my interests and skills .... ☐ ☐ ☐
- Considering alternative professions .... ☐ ☐ ☐
- Reaching out for interviews .... ☐ ☐ ☐
- Developing my CV and applying for jobs .... ☐ ☐ ☐
- Setting up a job shadowing .... ☐ ☐ ☐
- Volunteering in a new field .... ☐ ☐ ☐
- Upgrading my specialisation .... ☐ ☐ ☐
- Assessing the benefits of changing job (satisfaction, fulfilment,
  salary, stress, work-life balance) .... ☐ ☐ ☐
- Building confidence in my career options .... ☐ ☐ ☐
- Understanding psychometric tests used in recruitment .... ☐ ☐ ☐

            ☐ ☐ ☐

- Attending an entrepreneurship course .... ☐ ☐ ☐
- Identifying the team to ensure the essential business activities ☐ ☐ ☐
- Listing incubators and arrange meetings with their directors ... ☐ ☐ ☐
- Getting initial funding via FFF round (Family, Friends and Fools) ☐ ☐ ☐
- Preparing an elevator pitch .... ☐ ☐ ☐
- Getting to know businesses' legal and financial aspects .... ☐ ☐ ☐
- Creating, designing and registering a brand .... ☐ ☐ ☐
- Building a customer base .... ☐ ☐ ☐
- Defining how and what to communicate .... ☐ ☐ ☐
- Identifying the supply and distribution chains .... ☐ ☐ ☐
- Completing a Business Model Canvas and a Business Plan .... ☐ ☐ ☐
- Identifying interesting and possible investors .... ☐ ☐ ☐

            ☐ ☐ ☐

- Knowing my worth in the job market .... ☐ ☐ ☐
- Providing evidence of my value .... ☐ ☐ ☐
- Learning to deal with rejection .... ☐ ☐ ☐
- Refining the art of negotiation .... ☐ ☐ ☐
- Building a case for promotion .... ☐ ☐ ☐
- Evaluating the compromises attached to a raise (pains and gains) .. ☐ ☐ ☐
- Assessing my needs/values .... ☐ ☐ ☐
- Refining my emotional agility and resilience .... ☐ ☐ ☐
- _____ .... ☐ ☐ ☐
- _____ .... ☐ ☐ ☐
- _____ .... ☐ ☐ ☐
- _____ .... ☐ ☐ ☐

            ☐ ☐ ☐

The Economic, the Environmental and the Social impact contexts anticipate, respectively, the economic, the environmental and the social rewards and outcomes that *Humanity* will inherit from your project's solution and its implementation. You´ll assess the economic areas in which your projects may bring some kind of impact, or those in which some work toward optimisation would lead to some ways of economising (effort, time, space, finances, energy, etc). You will also look into how bio-centric, compostable, ethically sourced your projects are, and to what extent they may contribute to a sustainable condition for nature and biodiversity. And finally, you'll consider how humans can both rearrange their social interactions and better accept the cultural, religious and many other differences they encounter every day.

Naturally, your point of departure for this part of the exercise will be your current knowledge and precedents on these domains, which you can augment with a rapid collection of facts, keeping in mind that the time for hardcore research will come at a later stage, when you know what challenge you're committing to.

Note that these cards on the sustainability-led contexts of impact include cross-references to the UN's 17 Sustainable Development Goals (SDGs), so you can further explore possible routes of long-term and humanity-centred impact.

The Economic Card

ECONOMIC > DEVELOPING INVESTMENT	1	2	3
- Education	☐	☐	☐
- Infrastruture and Transport	☐	☐	☐
- Design	☐	☐	☐
- Data and Information	☐	☐	☐
- Technology	☐	☐	☐
- Communication and Media	☐	☐	☐
- Employment	☐	☐	☐
- Housing	☐	☐	☐
- Businesses and Marketing	☐	☐	☐
- Finance and Tax	☐	☐	☐
- Entertainment and Tourism	☐	☐	☐
- Health and Wellbeing	☐	☐	☐
	☐	☐	☐

Positive scores on this card will potentially contribute to the following SDGs. Identify them for each project.

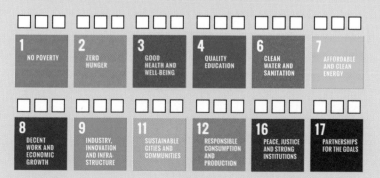

The Environmental Card

ENVIRONMENTAL > PLANET & SPECIES	1	2	3
- Reducing pollution and emissions	☐	☐	☐
- Decreasing waste	☐	☐	☐
- Contributing to the circularity of resources	☐	☐	☐
- Advancing neutral technologies	☐	☐	☐
- Mending climate conditions	☐	☐	☐
- Developing natural products	☐	☐	☐
- Balancing natural resources	☐	☐	☐
- Changing nutrition habits	☐	☐	☐
- Advancing/adopting renewable energies	☐	☐	☐
- Respecting biodiversity	☐	☐	☐
- Protecting and expanding animal rights	☐	☐	☐
- _____	☐	☐	☐
	☐	☐	☐

Positive scores on this card will potentially contribute to the following SDGs. Identify them for each project.

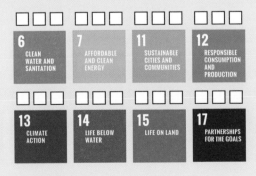

The Social Cards

SOCIAL > ADVANCED SOCIETY	1	2	3
- Developing citizenship	☐	☐	☐
- Designing education systems for all	☐	☐	☐
- Changing health and hygiene	☐	☐	☐
- Adjusting law and regulations	☐	☐	☐
- Enhancing culture	☐	☐	☐
- Rethinking structures of benefits	☐	☐	☐
- Adapting social behaviours to critical conditions	☐	☐	☐
- _____	☐	☐	☐
- _____	☐	☐	☐
- _____	☐	☐	☐
- _____	☐	☐	☐
- _____	☐	☐	☐
	☐	☐	☐

Positive scores on this card will potentially contribute to the
following SDGs. Identify them for each project.

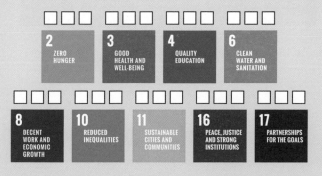

Improving:
- Accessibility and inclusivity .... ☐ ☐ ☐
- Gender and racial equality .... ☐ ☐ ☐
- Mobility .... ☐ ☐ ☐
- Empowerment of minorities .... ☐ ☐ ☐
- Parenthood and family .... ☐ ☐ ☐
- Work conditions/wellbeing .... ☐ ☐ ☐
- Quality in ageing .... ☐ ☐ ☐
- Quality in disability .... ☐ ☐ ☐
- Quality in disease or chronic condition .... ☐ ☐ ☐
- Respect toward ethnicity and religion .... ☐ ☐ ☐
- Awareness toward sexual orientation .... ☐ ☐ ☐

☐ ☐ ☐

Positive scores on this card will potentially contribute to the following SDGs. Identify them for each project.

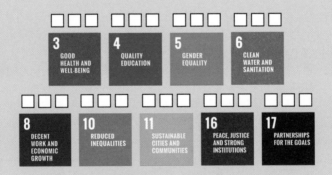

STEP 4

Try being scrupulous and honest about your own choices and evaluation. Unconscious biases are hard to overcome but the conscious ones should be put aside by all means. If you're working with a team, these can be easily observed: the kind of prejudice or inclination that tends to discriminate against certain groups of people or specific ways of doing/making/thinking.

An example of a bias that would undermine the purpose of **The Impact Plan** in the context of the example we have been using is the stigmatisation of leguminous grains as the food of the poor. Anyway, conscious or unconscious, when you're biased towards something or someone, you'll hardly make a fair judgment. It's not easy to be an impartial hero!

STEP 5

Whilst playing with the cards, you want to do some forecasting and speculative exercises. This is the time for you to actually put in practice the several approaches for the creation of scenarios discussed in Chapter 2. In general terms, there's a few questions you may want to ask (and answer) while completing the exercise on the following two pages:

- What are the main outcomes and implications that each of the five colourful impact contexts have on each of your short fictions?
- Are you building reactive or proactive scenarios? Or both?
- How would you navigate backwards should you be sometime far in a better future, assuming you achieved your goal and resolved the challenge you are about to pick?

Revisiting the Future

	EVOLUTION CASE	ALTERNATIVE CASE
🎓 1 2 3		
🚀 1 2 3		
🐷 1 2 3		
🍎 1 2 3		
⚙️ 1 2 3		

30 mn

Morcheeba
Tape Loop

EXCEPTION CASE	WHAT-IF

STEP 6

As you have probably noticed, once you have scored each of the stimuli of one card (either for one project only or for all), you add up the scores to find the card's total at the bottom. And, once you have all the applicable or relevant cards with totals for all the projects you're evaluating, it's time for you to add them all up and insert each project's total on the "Score" box, either on the Gauge Board or at the top of the canvas, depending on which you're using.

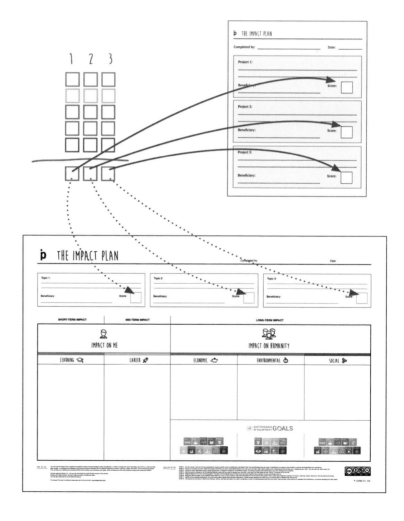

Pick the most impactful challenge and find the hidden gems of impact

STEP 7

The topic with the highest score is likely to be the most impactful and probably the one you should work on. Anyway, the obtained score is merely indicative because, after all the impact-centred thinking you've done up to this point, what really matters is your (and/or your team's) gut feeling about each of the scenarios you created. So, your goal remains oriented by the idea that, whatever the challenge, it must be PLEASURABLE, MEANINGFUL, AND IMPACTFUL.

STEP 8

Once you have a clear inclination toward one of the projects, move to the five colour-coded boards (or to the five colour-coded contexts of impact on the canvas). This is where you organise the respective colour stimuli that were very negatively (-2) or very positively (+2) scored in the context of the selected project. You can copy and write them down, you can create doodles that represent them or, if you're into crafts, you can cut them out from the downloadable version of the cards — so you avoid shredding your book — and glue them on the boards/canvas.

LEARNING

IMPACT ON YOU, THE HERO

SHORT-TERM OUTCOME

LEVEL OF ALTRUISM

Self-interest

CAREER

IMPACT ON YOU, THE HERO

MID-TERM OUTCOME

LEVEL OF ALTRUISM

Self-interest

ECONOMIC

IMPACT ON HUMANITY

LONG-TERM OUTCOME

LEVEL OF ALTRUISM

Life / Being

1 NO POVERTY	2 ZERO HUNGER	3 GOOD HEALTH AND WELL-BEING	4 QUALITY EDUCATION	6 CLEAN WATER AND SANITATION	7 AFFORDABLE AND CLEAN ENERGY
8 DECENT WORK AND ECONOMIC GROWTH	9 INDUSTRY, INNOVATION AND INFRA-STRUCTURE	11 SUSTAINABLE CITIES AND COMMUNITIES	12 RESPONSIBLE CONSUMPTION AND PRODUCTION	16 PEACE, JUSTICE AND STRONG INSTITUTIONS	17 PARTNERSHIPS FOR THE GOALS

ENVIRONMENTAL

IMPACT ON HUMANITY

LONG-TERM OUTCOME

LEVEL OF ALTRUISM

Life / Being

6 CLEAN WATER AND SANITATION	7 AFFORDABLE AND CLEAN ENERGY	11 SUSTAINABLE CITIES AND COMMUNITIES	12 RESPONSIBLE CONSUMPTION AND PRODUCTION
13 CLIMATE ACTION	14 LIFE BELOW WATER	15 LIFE ON LAND	17 PARTNERSHIPS FOR THE GOALS

SOCIAL

IMPACT ON HUMANITY

LONG-TERM OUTCOME

LEVEL OF ALTRUISM

Life / Being

2 ZERO HUNGER	3 GOOD HEALTH AND WELL-BEING	4 QUALITY EDUCATION	5 GENDER EQUALITY	6 CLEAN WATER AND SANITATION
8 DECENT WORK AND ECONOMIC GROWTH	10 REDUCED INEQUALITIES	11 SUSTAINABLE CITIES AND COMMUNITIES	16 PEACE, JUSTICE AND STRONG INSTITUTIONS	17 PARTNERSHIPS FOR THE GOALS

STEP 9 _____

The world is made of systems, and we need to shift our thinking to a more systematic way. This is precisely the moment when you identify all the possible implications, links and cause-effect relationships between the stimuli identified in Step 8, namely across contexts of impact (e.g. by drawing solid or dotted lines and arrows).

For example:

- If in **Learning** you scored negatively with -1 "Purchasing equipment and/or materials" it means you expect to have expenses for the duration of the challenge. Let's say you anticipate these costs may negatively impact your personal budget. But you can try to see beyond that: how does that connect to **Environmental**? How recyclable are these materials? What's their obsolescence plan? Is the cost to the planet of cutting down a tree to get that specific material being properly contemplated? And what about **Social** concerns? Where are these equipments made and what work conditions do those making them have? Is it the case that, after all, "Purchasing equipment and/or materials" should have been marked with -2?

- If in **Career** you scored positively "Volunteering in a new field" try to foresee the specifics of such field. Say you want to volunteer as teaching assistant at a primary school with the goal of developing children's awareness toward leguminous grains (yes, the Sicilian children from before). You may find this will have a small connection with your **Economic** card, under stimulus Education; it may link to a lot of stimuli on your **Environmental** card, and it may have some relationship with a few of the **Social** stimuli, such as "Designing education systems for all", "Changing health and hygiene" and "Adapting social behaviours to critical conditions".

To better to to view all these possible links, you may want to download the boards or the canvas from www.impact-plan.com.

Basically, this exercise follows a logic model... logic.

Lisa Wyatt Knowlton &
Cynthia C. Phillips
*The Logic Model
Guidebook: Better
Strategies for Great Results*

A logic model is a graphic representation depicting the theory of how an intervention of whatever nature produces its outcomes. It represents, in a simplified way, a 'theory of change' which is a tool grounded on a set of assumptions that explain both the actions that lead to the long-term goal (a better life for Humanity, in our case), and the connections between program activities and outcomes that occur at each step of the way (among other things, those related to You, the Hero).

Carol Weiss
*New Approaches to
Evaluating Comprehensive
Community Initiatives*

That said, by means of arrows, logic models represent the 'cause and effect' relationships between different aspects (stimuli) of your project. Remember that cause always comes before effect. For that reason, the stimuli on the boards or canvas should be arranged so that the arrows between them show how one stimulus (such as Understanding honesty and authenticity in Career) can be a cause of a subsequent stimulus (such as Developing citizenship in **Social**). Another example: you may want to evidence how some of the Learning stimuli related to cards "Creativity", "Pluridisciplinarity" and "Problem Solving" can have an effect on subsequent stimuli related to Career card "Entrepreneurship").

EntreComp: The
Entrepreneurship
Competence Framework
https://ec.europa.eu/social/

In short, you draw and visualise the possible interconnections between the five contexts of impact, anticipating the ecosystem of your **Impact Plan**. You will also develop a stronger inclination toward one or two of the SDGs, which will help you in better aligning your *ikigai*/purpose to the principles underpinning the selected challenge.

STEP 10

Use post-its of one colour to define the methods, techniques, actions, activities, and tasks you need to undertake in order to evidence/resolve the critical links you identified across the boards or contexts of impact on the canvas. This means you will be planning the HOW that will make you achieve your project goals. Use post-its of some other colour to represent, in your contexts of impact and scenarios' timeline, from short-term to long-term, the main milestones resulting from each action. Mapping all this out will hopefully lead you to the most impactful solutions — the WHAT. And if you remember Synek's Golden Circle mentioned a few pages ago, you get to the WHAT, after defining the HOW, and the latter only by knowing the WHY.

If you got this far, I regret to inform you that only now you managed to complete the *Determine* stage of your 'design process'. You're now ready to step into the Double Diamond.

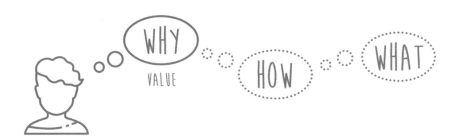

Notes, thoughts, drawings, ideas ...
Are you feeling overwhelmed? This is a great moment for some reflection-on-action. How much did you discover about yourself? How hard was it to identify the one challenge and how aligned are you with it?

(Yes, I reckon you may need some extra room for this end of chapter note taking...)

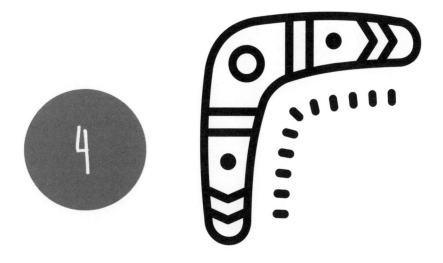

You, Yourself and Humanity

> *If you're gonna make it to the top, get a grip on this rock, and get a grip on yourself.*
> [Cheshire Cat]

A few months ago, I made a new friend in Brazil. You will probably think I'm mocking if I tell you that his name is *Batman*. Can you imagine? A super-hero? The thing is: Batman Zavareze is someone like you and me. He is a designer, new media artist and internationally recognised art director, who started his career at MTV Brasil in 1991 and worked with

Oliviero Toscani at Fabrica (the Benetton Group communications research centre), in Italy. At some point, as part of one of our chats, he said something that has been popping at the back of my head ever since: *as a society, we have been invested in reviewing, when what we really need is previewing.*

We've seen that previewing (what a good life in the future might look like) means knowing the WHY. I hope by now we can agree that, undoubtedly, knowing the WHY is important, but HOW and WHAT you do once you know your purpose is the actual challenge for all heroes like you (and me, and Batman). This is what Scott Goodson and Chip Walker refer to as the Purpose Gap, which is "the chasm between intentions and actions".

**Scott Goodson &
Chip Walker**
*Activate Brand Purpose:
how to harness the power
of movements to transform
your company*

So, despite this being a new (final) (and short) chapter, I invite you to look at the end of chapter 3, page 122. On the diagram at the bottom, basically what is being claimed is that the Value (WHY) must be the best-known variable when you face a Call to Adventure. Hence, it needs to be represented to the best extent to, subsequently, inform both the HOW and the WHAT. You assume that both the HOW and the WHAT (attached to whatever problem you may end up engaging with) are, to begin with, unknown: only the value/purpose, represented by the preferable *protopian* outcomes, and the impact that one wants to reach, are clear. Such representation of the WHY is precisely what
The Impact Plan helps you in achieving. In short, the WHY describes the purpose, it informs the rationale for taking up the project/activity, and is the backbone of the hero's speculative (previewing) process.

All this happens within the *Determine* stage. You may ask "How long does this stage last?". My answer is that its length very much depends on the kind of challenges and briefs you contemplate, and the deadlines you are given to make a decision regarding which one to work on.

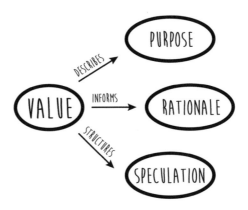

Then, when you feel ready to initiate the Double Diamond process (or any other project development process, for that matter), you want to keep a sound experience, so you can go beyond the *Determine* stage and decide which challenge to choose. Only after that you start the reunion of all the resources and skills necessary to avoid the Purpose Gap. Or — what I tell my students — to avoid shutting your good intentions and promising projects inside a dark (and disorganised) drawer. Please no, don't do that!

As you can see on the next two pages, **The Impact Plan** is just one tool that promotes the craft of thinking and that is part of a much bigger ecosystem, filled with other accessories, techniques and resources that will help you move on to find your best approaches (HOW) and both the ideation and the development of possible outputs (WHAT). WHY, HOW and WHAT, are constantly interwoven and feeding each other. Their relationship depends on how you approach your project and how often you intend to review your rationale, compare your assumptions with your ideas and possible solutions, and revisit the card's stimuli to help you define your unique value proposition (or the KPI's you'll need to monitor the success of your project). That's why you may find yourself using **The Impact Plan** in other moments that go way beyond the *Determine* stage.

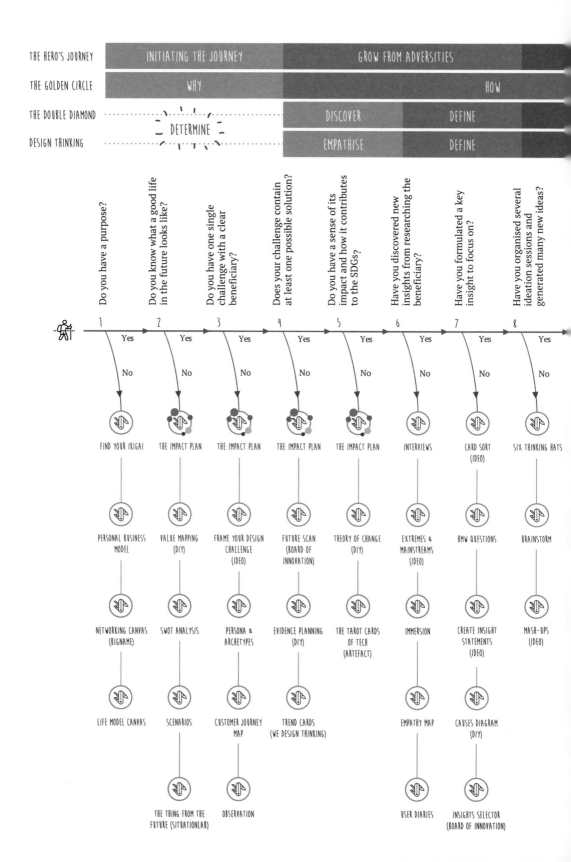

THE HERO'S JOURNEY	INITIATING THE JOURNEY	GROW FROM ADVERSITIES	
THE GOLDEN CIRCLE	WHY	HOW	
THE DOUBLE DIAMOND	DETERMINE	DISCOVER	DEFINE
DESIGN THINKING	DETERMINE	EMPATHISE	DEFINE

Do you have a purpose?

Do you know what a good life in the future looks like?

Do you have one single challenge with a clear beneficiary?

Does your challenge contain at least one possible solution?

Do you have a sense of its impact and how it contributes to the SDGs?

Have you discovered new insights from researching the beneficiary?

Have you formulated a key insight to focus on?

Have you organised several ideation sessions and generated many new ideas?

1 2 3 4 5 6 7 8

Yes / No (for each step 1–8)

1 FIND YOUR IKIGAI
2 THE IMPACT PLAN
3 THE IMPACT PLAN
4 THE IMPACT PLAN
5 THE IMPACT PLAN
6 INTERVIEWS
7 CARD SORT (IDEO)
8 SIX THINKING HATS

PERSONAL BUSINESS MODEL
VALUE MAPPING (DIY)
FRAME YOUR DESIGN CHALLENGE (IDEO)
FUTURE SCAN (BOARD OF INNOVATION)
THEORY OF CHANGE (DIY)
EXTREMES & MAINSTREAMS (IDEO)
HMW QUESTIONS
BRAINSTORM

NETWORKING CANVAS (BIGNAME)
SWOT ANALYSIS
PERSONA & ARCHETYPES
EVIDENCE PLANNING (DIY)
THE TAROT CARDS OF TECH (ARTEFACT)
IMMERSION
CREATE INSIGHT STATEMENTS (IDEO)
MASH-UPS (IDEO)

LIFE MODEL CANVAS
SCENARIOS
CUSTOMER JOURNEY MAP
TREND CARDS (WE DESIGN THINKING)
EMPATHY MAP
CAUSES DIAGRAM (DIY)

THE THING FROM THE FUTURE (SITUATIONLAB)
OBSERVATION
USER DIARIES
INSIGHTS SELECTOR (BOARD OF INNOVATION)

Have you identified the most promising idea and defined assumptions for a solution?

Have you prototyped your most likely solution?

Have you tested your prototype with representatives of your beneficiary?

Did you validate the solution, namely against your purpose and a *good life* in the future?

Do you have a clear UVP and KPIs to monitor/measure your solution's impact?

Do you have a dissemination plan?

Have you got buy-in from key stakeholders?

Have you identified the key partners that will fund and help implement your solution?

10   11   12   13   14   15   16

Yes   Yes   Yes   Yes   Yes   Yes   Yes   Yes

No   No   No   No   No   No   No   No

THE IMPACT PLAN | STORYBOARD & MOODBOARD | LIVE PROTOTYPING | FEEDBACK LOOPS | THE IMPACT PLAN | THOUGHT STARTERS | PITCH (IDEO) | BUSINESS MODEL CANVAS (STRATEGYSER)

SIGN PRINCIPLES (IDEO) | ROLE PLAYING (IDEO) | HOW-NOW-WOW MATRIX | UNIQUE VALUE PROPOSITION CANVAS (STRATEGYSER) | ROADMAP (IDEO) | WAYS TO GROW FRAMEWORK (IDEO)

GUT CHECK (IDEO) | RAPID PROTOTYPING | MONITOR & EVALUATE (IDEO) | RESOURCE ASSESSMENT (IDEO)

SCENARIOS | PROTOTYPE TESTING PLAN (DIY) | VISION CARD (BOARD OF INNOVATION)

RVICE BLUEPRINT

The ecosystem and the eternal return

On the previous two pages you can see that **The Impact Plan** is mostly present in the *Determine* stage, which corresponds to the moment in which one both seeks answers to the WHY (Sinek's Golden Circle), and initiates the Hero Journey. In fact, should we consider these two narrative-based models, you'll see that the tool can be of use in their remaining stages as well:

- In answering HOW, namely when 1) considering how the then already selected challenge/project contributes to the SDGs [5] — this is an example of when the hero Grows from Adversities, and 2) how the most promising idea aligns to the definition of assumptions for a solution [9]— which happens when the hero Assembles a Team of Allies;
- In answering WHAT, to support the creation of a clear unique value proposition (UVP), to work as a benchmark for future comparison and to help you gather the key performance indicators (KPIs) that will be used to monitor/measure the impact and sucess of the achieved solution [13] — when the hero contemplates his/her return and the ways in which Giving Back to Society can actually happen).

Throughout the journey, and to support you in all different stages, you will find yourself resorting to many other tools and techniques, which have been mapped out for your convenience. You will find all of them with a very simple search in the Internet, but in some cases I thought it could be useful to direct you either to their creators (IDEO, Strategyser, Board of Innovation, BigName, Artefact, We Design Thinking and SituationLab), or to some of the most hero-friendly templates (Nesta's DIY Toolkit).

The Impact Plan also works as a supporting instrument for the reappraisal and recalibration of any entity's vision and direction, since the constant return to a *Determine* stage is most beneficial — if not for other reasons, because things around us change all the time.

And then, what?

The UN's SDGs are to be achieved by 2030. Now, let's face it. We are roughly seven years away from there. And that is more or less halfway since the SDGs have been released. Some work has been done but, unless something beautiful and magical has been kept for the second half and is just about to happen, the time we have left feels like totally insufficient to tick all the 17 boxes.

Obviously, no one truly anticipated the recent events that have somehow reset the timer — which aftermaths have been having a huge negative impact on our efforts towards the SDGs. The COVID-19 pandemic brought a lot of unexpected issues that increased the difficulties in achieving some of the UN's sustainable development goals, namely SDG 1: "End poverty in all its forms everywhere". The fact that many businesses couldn't survive the successive lockdowns brought a global rise of unemployment which led to the escalation of inequalities, particularly detrimental to the most vulnerable. On top of this, the Russia/Ukraine conflict: besides the increased numbers of refugees, migrants, or displaced and emotionally distressed individuals, the boost in prices of goods as simple as bread are potentially triggering a global food crisis. And all this whilst so many other places in the world remain, consistently but less broadcast, at some sort of war. How on planet Earth are we supposed to resolve SDG1 in such a short period of time?

The truth is 2030 is around the corner. We must think and act fast. And, regardless of our protopian and successful achievement of all goals, we must think beyond that.

Kings of Convenience
*I don't know what I can
save you from*

Other problems will develop and new goals will be recommended after 2030. Unless we are dominated by some utterly superior and advanced species, able to contradict or invert the laws of physics that regulate our lives on this planet, the world will not become a static place where, suddenly, the attained "hurray" state means "now-that-we-solved-all-the-problems-let's-not-move-a-thing-or-even-breathe-for-that-matter". Should such a state be reached, it wouldn't mean human beings would become less... human. I think I mentioned before that we're naturally lazy, and that we've also been partially hardwired to selfishness.

How common-good is all this?

The way we define our ideas of what is right and wrong have been historically influenced mostly by two streams: the traditional moral discourse, based on religious sermons and philosophical views, and the one brought to us by the advancements in the biological and social sciences, being economics chief among the latter.

Darwin's evolutionary and biological diversity theories defended that natural selection occurred among those that evidenced "fitness". This meant species were instinctively searching for number ones and alphas in order to prosper and survive. Since the less fit would be naturally swept away, one had to be "naturally" selfish. Later on, and focusing on the human species only, Herbert Simon, Nobel in Economic Sciences, explained that, when having to make a decision (and in reference to decision-makers in organisations), individuals contemplate what lies before them researching the range of alternatives they face, not only at that moment but also those in the future. He also said they follow this sort of self-interested goal which is to maximise their gain in any conceivable situation — basically the "what's in it for me" posture that comes with the "hedonistic calculus" proposed by Neel Burton and which I mentioned in chapter 1. When you focus on your individual rights and gains, you're usually thinking in a short-term perspective and deprioritising the common good, which is normally long-term-led.

Amitai Etzioni has proposed the idea of a dual human nature, both selfish and altruistic by turns, where individuals face this permanent conflict between their commitments to moral values and the common good, and their self-interest. Professor emeritus of Economics Robert Frank comes up with the *commitment model* to explain good behaviour based on the logic of self-interest, defending that those who are seen as trustworthy will accrue gains almost immediately, suggesting that there's always *something in it for us* if we're honest. I guess we all agree it is very difficult to ask people to sacrifice their freedom and some of their self-interests for the sake of the "common good". But I also believe it is consensual that any nudge toward considering the common good (and to me, the planet is our biggest and most shared *good in common*) urge us to think on the kind of society we want so we can concretise our idea of a "good life" in the future. It also makes us think on how we are supposed to get there, considering that we are all members of the same Earthean community and that, whilst we want to preserve our own freedom, we must also respect and value the freedom of our planet fellows.

Amitai Etzioni
Happiness is the Wrong Metric: A Liberal Communitarian Response to Populism

Robert Frank
Passions Within Reason

The Clash
Should I stay or should I go

So, for most of us, until we, as a typically individualistic society, evolve into something different, we all can find room in our lives to help the others, provided we have enough room for our own movements. That's what underpins **The Impact Plan**. It's a tool that moves away from the *Me, Myself and I* kind of attitude (which is all but heroic), proposing that whilst focusing on *Me, Myself and Humanity*, one can actually surface honest concerns towards the sustainability of our planet. And do something PLEASURABLE, MEANINGFUL AND IMPACTFUL about it!

Debriefing the journey

At this point, I have ten pieces of advice in what regards anticipating the impact of possible heroic adventures, and getting the best from using **The Impact Plan**:

1. **Be realistic in your expectations**: you don't need to have a very precise vision of what the outcomes of your projects may be, but you should have a good sense of where they may take you in the short, medium, and long run — so you can choose the best one for you, in that moment of your life.

2. **Keep a question in front of you at all times**: *What if* and *How might we* questions are great. As you progress through the different colourful contexts of impact, and as you get to better define your expectations against your own purpose, you may find yourself naturally asking this sort of questions. They will simply come to you.

3. **Plan your projects' impact in a network map kind of way**. As your questions start giving you possible and tentative answers, use the boards (or the canvas) to surface relations between everything that may look like a node: a stimulus, a motivation, a capacity, a skill that needs to be developed, an ambition, an opportunity to travel, a destination, a person you will meet, a person you want to keep close and love, a perception of value, a cost, a likely deadline. Camilla Pang elucidates why working with a network diagram can be so useful: "... because it's dynamic, capable of adapting as your circumstances do. It's clarifying, helping us to understand

Camilla Pang
Explaining Humans: What Science Can Teach Us about Life, Love and Relationships

what is and isn't truly important. And it's focused on connectivity — allowing us to see the things that are linked, which nodes are influencing or being influenced, and where a certain path may lead". Besides all this, you also develop a holistic understanding of how you can be a true hero contributing to a better world.

4. Take short and quick notes of every insightful or relevant realisation you make during the journey and throughout your project. After the completion of the challenge, the road back to the Ordinary World is a bumpy one, in the sense that the hero will be recollecting all the events, processes, people and resources he/she experienced during the challenge. All that will be part of the story the hero will be asked to tell as soon as he/she "arrives" from the journey. A publication, a report, a diary, a piece of art, a manifesto, an informal chat over a coffee — in some way or another, all the way from the Call to Adventures (e.g. receiving the client briefs) to the encounter with the Elixir or Treasure (the identified and validated solution) will have to be told and shared with the others.

5. Make it flexible. If you feel not all cards are needed, don't use them (it would be the same as marking their stimuli as zero). If you want to start by anticipating the impact on your Career and then move backwards to Learning and only after that consider the Sustainability impact contexts, that'll do as much as in any other order. If you find that using both boards and canvas makes sense to you, go for it! If you feel comfortable with using the canvas/board only and not the cards, that's absolutely fine.

6　Listen to your gut feeling — scores based on numbers are great but... they're just numbers. If a project scores higher than the one you're leaning to, you may want to sleep over it and check whether next day your guts still whisper. If they do, you probably want to forget about the quantitative scores. As an alternative to numbers, you may want to define a scoring system based on visual signs with some sort of qualitative meaning: stars, emojis, colours as in traphic lights... There's plenty of room for creativity.

7　Don't waste your time. Because, when your gut feeling's voice is undeniably strong, that means you may not need **The Impact Plan** at all — you instantaneously know what challenge to go for.

8　If the hero is a brand, you may want to reach out, because an organisational version of the tool is being developed.

9　Look around you and resort to what geography gives you. Ibn Khaldun, a muslim Arab sociologist and political philosopher from the 14th century, said that "Geography is Destiny". Although controversial, I must say I don't think geography alone determines the fate of a society as a whole. But each place on Earth has its own unique characteristics (some obvious and visible, and others less so) that can be used for innovation. And if you want your project and solution to be sustainable, you want to avoid unecessary economic, environmental and social costs. **Saving the world globally will only happen with localised action.**

10 Get to know the Museum of Happiness. A local physical visit is easy if/when you're in or near London. You can also take a peek at their website (which doesn't look great, but is full of inspiring good intentions). Basically the advice here is to reflect on their main goal, which is:

Museum of Happiness
*https://www.
museumofhappiness.org*

DISCOVERING THE ART AND SCIENCE OF SUSTAINABLE HAPPINESS.

Wouldn't this be the most beautiful 18th SDG in the UN's list? I gave it a try and designed its icon; it could look like this:

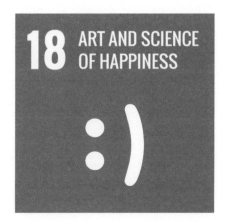

Notes, thoughts, drawings, ideas ...
Yes, this page was thought for you to start the debrief of your jouney.

So, thank you (again)!

This is something that usually happens when our heroes return safe and sound from their adventures: we develop a feeling of gratitude and we thank whoever we believe was responsible for their success.

Hence, I want to thank you, again:

- For having read this book.
- For engaging with its proposed activities.
- For listening to the music I suggested throughout — I hope you liked it and found some new stuff for your own playlists!
- For putting yourself in a hero's boots and empathising with the world and its gifts.
- For agreeing that we must not only look into the future but we must indeed do something about it — even if we think it's insignificant.
- Or, for disagreeing with the whole book, for that matter — if we were all in agreement, heroes wouldn't be needed, challenges wouldn't appear and causes wouldn't exist. And the world would be a monochromatic place. And I like colours. All of them.

Max Richter
Spring 1 - Recomposed:
Vivaldi's Four Seasons

I also want to thank some people who had a big deal of impact on this book and on the development of **The Impact Plan** as a tool:

First, my ex-co-author, Patrick Roberts. Patrick is my most impactful colleague ever, and he was the first person (other than me) to use the tool. He was also the biggest source of PLEASURABLE, MEANINGFUL AND IMPACTFUL contributions to this book, which he agreed to co-author until he decided he wouldn't — despite me trying to convince him otherwise. But he was meant to be a hero at some other challenge and I had to let him go.

Secondly, I must dedicate a word to all my MA students at the University of West London. Some of them never had any contact with **The Impact Plan**, but they were, without knowing, making me aware of its relevance. Others used it in its original, ugly and very incomplete form, confirming that it made sense as a sort of project selection haven. The others used it in its refined, high fidelity first version, which I had to rush due to COVID-19 kicking in, and assessment strategies having to be fully rethought and reviewed for remote ways of being.

Donald Norman
Design for a Better
World

Of course, I have to thank David Pearl, for his detailed feedback on the tool, which he kindly provided when **The Impact Plan** still was a rough paper-based mock-up of what we have today. I am also grateful for Don Norman's generous words of support and for his willingness to write them, since I first reached out. I very much look forward to reading his new book, *Design for a Better World*. And, a word to my dearest aunty Guida, who's the greatest storyteller in my life, who's always up for challenges and who proofread this book — which means, if you find any weird phrasal stuff or spelling mistakes, I'll have to ask her to re-review the next edition.

Finally, I want to thank all the people who downloaded **The Impact Plan** and gave it some useful use, namely those who invited me to deliver workshops and those who attended them — and with whom I learned so much. Thank you!

Bibliography

This is the list of all the other sources that were not referenced in the text body but that were part of the corpus. If not for other purpose, they were most inspirational!

Beck, U. (1992). *Risk Society: Towards a New Modernity*. Sage.

Berger, D. & Wild, C. (2017). Enhancing student performance and employability through the use of authentic assessment techniques in extra and co-curricular activities (ECCAs), *The Law Teacher*, 51(4), 428-439.

Curedale, R. (2013). *Design Thinking: process and methods manual*. Design Community College.

Damásio, A. (2006). *Descartes' Error: Emotion, Reason and the Human Brain*. Vintage Publishing.

Dorst, K. (2011). The core of 'design thinking' and its application. *Design Studies*, 32(6), 521–532.

Duckworth, A. L., Matthews, M. D., Kelly, D. R. & Peterson, C. (2007). Grit: Perseverance and Passion for Long-Term Goals. *Journal of Personality and Social Psychology*, 92(6), 1087– 1101.

Dunne, A. & Raby, F. (2013). Speculative Everything - Design, Fiction, and Social Dreaming, Cambridge, MA: The MIT Press.

Dunne, D. & Martin, R. (2006). Design thinking and how it will change management education: an interview and discussion. *Academy of Management Learning & Education*, 5(4), 512– 523.

Future of Design Education (2020). *The Future of Design Education Initiative Overview*, December 2020. Retrieved on 28/02/2022 from https://www.futureofdesigneducation.org

Giddens, A. (1991). *Modernity and Self-Identity: Self and Society in the Late Modern Age*. Polity Press.

Giddens, A. (1993). *New Rules of Sociological Method*. Stanford University Press.

Jackson, D. (2016). Re-conceptualising graduate employability: the importance of pre-professional identity. *Higher Education Research & Development*, 35 (5), 925-939.

Kieslinger, B., Pata, K. & Fabian, C. M. (2009). A Participatory Design Approach for the Support of Collaborative Learning and Knowledge Building in Networked Organizations. *International Journal of Advanced Corporate Learning*, 2, 34-38.

Lelis, C. (2021). Optimised Taxonomy for the Analysis and Design of Canvas-Based Tools. In: Martins N., Brandão D. (eds) *Advances in Design and Digital Communication*. Digicom 2020. Springer Series in Design and Innovation, vol 12., pp 205-215, Springer. https://doi.org/10.1007/978-3-030-61671-7_19

Leman, J. (2018). *Postgraduate Taught Experience Survey 2018*. Advance HE.

Lundmark, L.W., Nickerson, J.A. & Derrick, D. (2017). Wicked Problem Formulation: Models of Cognition in the Design and Selection of Valuable Strategies. *Academy of Management 2017 Proceedings*, Vol 1, 17551.

Maslow, A. H. (1943). A theory of human motivation. *Psychological Review*, 50(4), 370–396.

Persson, D., Erlandsson, L-K., Eklund, M. & Iwarsson, S. (2001). Value dimensions, meaning, and complexity in human occupation - a tentative structure for analysis. *Scandinavian Journal of Occupational Therapy*, 8, 7–18.

QAA (2009). *Personal development planning: guidance for institutional policy and practice in higher education*. Retrieved on 04/11/2019 from https://www.qaa.ac.uk

Rennie, D. L. (1992). Qualitative analysis of the client's experience of psychotherapy: The unfolding of reflexivity. In S. G. Toukmanian, & D. L. Rennie (Eds.), *Psychotherapy process research: Paradigmatic and narrative approaches* (pp. 211–233). Sage.

Savickas, M. L. (2016). Reflection and reflexivity during life-design interventions: Comments on Career Construction Counseling. *Journal of Vocational Behavior*, 97, 84-89.

Tharp, B. M. & Tharp, S. M. (2018). *Discursive Design: Critical, Speculative and Alternative Things*. MIT Press.

The Design Council (2021). *What is the framework for innovation? Design Council's evolved Double Diamond*. Retrieved from https://www.designcouncil.org.uk/news-opinion/what-framework-innovation-design-councils-evolved-double-diamond

Ward, R. & Watts, A. G. (2009). Personal development planning and employability, in Personal development planning and employability. Learning and Employability Series. Higher Education Academy. Retrieved on 31/01/2020, from https://www.heacademy.ac.uk/system/files/pdp_and_employability_jan_2009.pdf

Watts, A.G. (2006). *Career Development Learning and Employability*. Learning and Employability Series Two, n.5. Higher Education Academy. Retrieved from https://www.heacademy.ac.uk/system/files/esect_career_development_learning_and_employability.pdf

Zwick, M. & Fletcher, J. A. (2014). Levels of Altruism. *Biological Theory*, 9, 100-107.